Dedication

To Marvin and Donna,
my parents.
Thanks.

Contents

INTRODUCTION

Talk About Stress!

While I was writing this book, the following things happened:

- Both my kids got chicken pox.
- We had torrential rainfall and—for the first time anyone in the neighborhood can remember—all the basements on our street flooded. About a foot and a half of water. Our family room is in the basement.
- As a result of the flooding I had to fix the washing machine, dryer, water heater, furnace, television, videocassette recorder and typewriter. Also, all of my old Beatles albums were ruined. I haven't listened to them in years, but it's the principle of the thing.
- The water bed my wife and I bought on a lark seven years ago sprung a leak. And we can't find the hole. So we had to move into Sarah's room while she took the extra bed in Ben's room.
- Something went wrong with the commode, and it makes a funny noise every time it's flushed. And it's still doing it.
- The lawn mower quit running right in the middle of the front yard. So now I have the only lawn on the street with a Mohawk haircut.
- My youngest brother got married. It was an epic family blowout that lasted three days. I was the officiating pastor at the wedding.
- My mortgage payment was increased 10 percent.

●

I tell all this not to gain your sympathy—though that

would be nice. Rather, I share it so you'll know that I don't speak of stress from some stress-free ivory tower. I have my share of stress. Just like you.

But I also have something else. Something that has taught me a great deal about the stresses of parenting a teenager: 18 years of experience as a youth minister.

In those 18 years, I've spent thousands of hours with teenagers not unlike your own. I've led them, taught them, played with them, listened to them, counseled them and prayed with them.

I've also become friends with and been counselor to many parents of teenagers. I've wept with them, laughed with them, thought and pondered with them, and prayed with them.

What should we do?

What do you think?

Is my kid normal?

Am I doing the right thing?

I've seen some parents blossom as their kids moved through adolescence. But I've seen others burn themselves out from the stress of parenting a teenager.

► *Feeling the Stress*

In working with kids and their parents, I've noticed that the stresses they feel are often predictable. And if parents and kids know to anticipate them, they might be better prepared. And maybe more parents and kids could enjoy adolescence and grow together instead of apart during those wonderful years.

So—this book.

Fixing Your Frazzled Family begins by looking at stress and how it affects you and your family. We'll look at why adolescence is so stressful—for both the teenager and the family.

Then we'll discuss the special, specific stresses of families with teenagers: time, money, conflict, changing relationships and change. I'll suggest specific ways you and your family can deal with these stresses in a positive, Christian way.

Finally, the book concludes by suggesting ways to reduce and avoid stress in your family life.

► *Celebrating the Joy*

I hope *Fixing Your Frazzled Family* helps you in your relationship with your teenager. I hope you'll discover ways to relate to each other and to make your family stronger.

I hope you'll share the stories. Read them to each other and realize that, hey, you aren't alone. Lots of people feel the same things you're feeling. And I hope you'll add some stories of your own.

I also hope that 10 or 15 years from now, as you sit around the kitchen table, you'll retell the stories of your kids' teenage years. As you do so, you'll laugh and cry and feel good about yourself and your kids.

If you do that, this book will have served its purpose. And I will have served mine.

CHAPTER 1

Unraveling the Stress Mess

"I don't know what happened! I mean everything was going so well, and all of a sudden . . . *boom*!"

Mary was sitting in my office, clutching a tissue in her hand. She wasn't crying. But she apparently wanted to be ready.

I asked her to continue.

"Our family's schedule is so crazy. It always has been. We're active people, you know. Work, church, school, scouts, swimming lessons, piano lessons, sports, plays, band, choir, babysitters, meetings . . . just everything. But we've always managed to stay on top of it . . . until now."

"Until now?"

"We were like a team, you know—our whole family. We all sort of took care of each other. Clarise could cook a complete meal when she was 10. Sometimes I'd get home from work and she'd have vacuumed—and done laundry even. Teamwork."

As she paused to let out her breath, I was thinking something must be different now.

"But it's different now."

Ah.

So we began searching for what was different. Something drastic that just sort of slipped up on everyone without warning.

"What about Darren? Is he being difficult?"

"No, Darren's fine," she explained. "He's 9 and into Cub Scouts, soccer and Daredevil comics." Same old Darren.

"What about Melissa?"

"No. Melissa's 7. She's into Cabbage Patch dolls. Piano lessons. Brownies." Same old Melissa.

"What about you and Jerry? Has something changed between you?"

"I don't think so. Sometimes it doesn't seem like we see much of each other . . . you know, working 10 hours a day, five or six days a week," she mused. "But that's not new. We've been doing that for 12 years."

So that must leave . . . Clarise. "How old is Clarise?" I inquired.

"Well, she just turned 14 three months ago and . . ."

Bingo!

"It's like Jekyll and Hyde," Mary said. "One day she helps, and it's like the old days. The next day she snaps at everyone and locks herself in her room. She talks on the phone for hours, plays her stereo so loud the windows rattle . . . I dunno. She's pouty one minute, cheerful the next . . . I think I'm losing my mind."

It took a while, but I managed to assure Mary she wasn't losing her mind. She was experiencing something thousands of families experience every year: a teenager.

With a little thoughtful and prayerful preparation—and the willingness to work hard as parents—Mary and Jerry will not only survive their daughter's adolescence, but they may even thrive in it.

► *Finding the Stress*

Face it: Life is stressful. Money, sex, love, friends, work—even play—all bring stress into our lives. Of course, some things bring more stress than others. And some families experience more stress than others.

But you can't avoid it. Everyone has to cope with stress.

What about your family? What kind of stress are you under right now? The "Family Stress Test" (page 14) is a simple way to help you measure your family's stress level.

Common Stresses in Families

Family expert Dolores Curran researched families across the United States and found the following are the top 10 causes of stress in families:

1. Economics/finances/budgeting
2. Children's behavior/discipline/sibling fighting
3. Insufficient couple time
4. Lack of shared responsibility in the family
5. Communicating with children
6. Insufficient "me" time
7. Guilt for not accomplishing more
8. Spousal relationship
9. Insufficient family playtime
10. Overscheduled family calendar

Dolores Curran, *Stress and the Healthy Family* (San Francisco: Harper & Row, 1985) 20.

► *Dealing With the Stress*

Where stress is concerned, the world isn't divided into "haves" and "have nots." Some families are rich in stress and some are poor, but we all have it. Sure, you can avoid or put off some stress. But you can't escape it.

So you have to cope with it.

As humans, we're designed to cope with stress in clear, identifiable ways. Unlike opossums, we don't freeze up under stress. Neither do we stampede like cattle.

God created us to handle stress. Our bodies react immediately to stressful situations. The stress reaction was impressed into our ancestors thousands of years ago and is still there, waiting to act whenever needed. "Steering the Stress Wheel" explains how our bodies respond to stress.

► *Understanding How Stress Can Hurt*

Our ability to cope with stress is remarkably helpful. Emergency room doctors and nurses, paramedics, police officers, soldiers, athletes and most people in emergency situations rely on it to pull them through.

In moderate doses—well-spaced and well-timed—stress

Family Stress Test

Read the following list of events, and circle the number after each event that has occurred in your immediate family in the past 24 months.

A parent dies. 100
Parents divorce. 73
A child leaves home. 65
A family member dies. 63
A parent is arrested. 63
A parent is injured or seriously ill. 53
A teenager begins driving. 50
The primary breadwinner loses job. 47
A child is arrested. 45
A family member is caught using drugs. 45
A child is injured or seriously ill. 44
A child is caught using alcohol. 40
Parents have sex difficulties. 39
A new member joins the family. 39
A teenage child becomes pregnant. 39
A teenage child becomes a father. 38
Family finances change drastically. 38
A close friend of a family member dies. 37
The primary breadwinner changes occupation. 36
A mortgage or loan is foreclosed on. 36
Parents have a loud or serious argument. .35
Parents and children have a loud or serious argument. 31
The primary breadwinner gets a promotion. 30
Family discovers a teenager is sexually active. 29
Family has trouble with in-laws. 29
A parent disagrees with teenager's choice of friends. 28
A child participates in three or more extracurricular activities at once. 26
A family member quits smoking. 25
The primary breadwinner has trouble with a boss. 23
The primary breadwinner faces radical changes at work. 20
Family moves. 20
A child has trouble in school. 20
Family joins or leaves a church. 18
A teenager breaks up with a sweetheart. .17
A child participates in organized sports. .16
Family routine changes significantly. 15
A family member goes on a diet. 15
Family takes a vacation. 13
Extended family gets together at Christmas. 13
Siblings fight more than three times each month. 11

continued

Now add other stresses your family experiences that aren't on the list. To score them, compare the stress level to other indicators on the list and choose an appropriate number to write in the right column.

Then add together all the numbers you circled plus the ones you added.

____ ______

____ ______

____ ______

____ ______

Total score: ______

If your score is more than 300—Take immediate action to reduce the stress in your family. If you don't, arguments will get louder and longer, feelings will get more profound, time will seem endless and someone—probably a parent—will get sick or injured. Quickly read the rest of the book, join an exercise class and take a day off.

If your score is 200 to 300—Your stress is on the high side, but you're surviving. This book will give you lots of ideas on ways to make the stress more manageable.

If your score is 50 to 200—You're experiencing normal stress levels. Things go well sometimes, sometimes they don't. Use this book as a guide to managing stress.

If your score is less than 50—Gather the family in the living room and take everyone's pulse—just to make sure everyone still has one!

Steering the Stress Wheel

1. The body mobilizes energy. At the first sign of stress, organs within your body jump into action to mobilize your energy. Oxygen, sugar and fat are dumped into the bloodstream. Hormones go to work.

2. The body consumes energy. Your heart beats faster. Blood surges into your muscles, making you stronger and faster. Your five senses become more acute. You begin to breathe deeper and faster, and unnecessary activities cease—you stop digesting food and your sexual instincts are squelched. Also, your pain threshold rises and your mind is hard at work figuring out how to respond.

3. You act. No, that's too mild. Let's say you explode into a flurry of activity. You feel an almost overwhelming urge to *do something*! Doctors tell us our most overwhelming instinct is to flee. However, when flight isn't possible, we fight and protect ourselves.

4. Your body returns to normal. Finally, when the stress-inducing occasion has been successfully driven off or you've safely escaped from it, your body returns to normal. Energy reserves are replenished, heart rate slows down, senses dull, digestion and sexual drive return, and you breathe normally. You're ready for the next stress.

makes life interesting and exciting. All those hormones pumping through our bodies make us more productive, faster, smarter, more creative and generally happier. Moderate stress relieves boredom and makes life, well . . . spicy.

However, if we get too much stress or it isn't well-timed, it can have just the opposite effect. It can make us weak, slow, dense, angry, mean, tired, withdrawn, run-down and even ill.

Stress can affect us negatively in three ways.

Too much stress—If we get too much stress in too short a time, our bodies can't cope with it all. The organs that supply energy don't have time to refill themselves, and there's no energy reserve to tap. We call people in this condition burned out or used up. If something doesn't happen to reduce the stress in their lives, they become physically ill, depressed or even suicidal.

Poorly channeled stress—Often, the problem isn't that we have too much stress, but that we don't deal well with the stress we have. Running away from the stress or fighting to overcome it are our first reactions. But these two options rarely help with family stress and the stress we encounter with our children. There are several reasons:

- First, because we're parents—Fighting with or fleeing from our children may be unavoidable from time to time. But these responses aren't the best ways to deal with our kids.
- Second, because we're human—While our instincts may tell us to fight or flee, we must often ignore our instincts and force ourselves to reason our way through a crisis.
- And third, because we're Christians—Jesus doesn't fight his enemies, nor does he flee from them. He embraces them. And he tells us to do the same: "You have heard that it was said, 'You shall love your neighbor and hate your enemy.' But I say to you, Love your enemies and pray for those who persecute you" (Matthew 5:43-44).

If our Lord would have us love and embrace our enemies, can we do less for our children? For parents, then, stress is harmful when it's channeled only toward fighting and fleeing because we forget to channel it toward loving.

Negative coping techniques—Finally, stress hurts us when we cope with it in a negative or harmful way. Fighting and fleeing may hurt sometimes, but sometimes they're necessary. Other responses, however, are never helpful and only rush us toward burnout, despair and the sickbed. Instead of easing the stress, they add to it.

And when we fail to use positive coping techniques—such as exercise and hugs—that adds to the stress too. The "How Do You Cope?" box helps you evaluate the ways you cope with stress.

As you see from the box, negative coping methods add to your stress. They may seem to help ease the pain, but the respite is only temporary. In reality, they make the total stress higher.

► *Feeling Guilty . . . When We Don't Need To*

Admitting the stress in our families isn't always easy. As parents we watch TV shows about perfect families, and we wonder what's wrong with us. Why does our family feel so much stress? Why do we always seem so busy and get so little done? Why do we have so much trouble with our kids' stress?

Somehow, somewhere we've gotten the message that family life should be easy, fun, stress-free and fulfilling. And if it isn't, something terrible must be wrong.

What's wrong may not be our family, but our perspective. We forget some basic assumptions about parenting. Once we accept these assumptions, we'll be better prepared to deal constructively with the stress in our families.

Assumption #1: Parenting a teenager is stressful. Teenagers naturally try to separate themselves from us. And any time someone tries to break away from the family it's stressful.

The natural stress of the changing relationship is enough. Feeling guilty about that stress is counterproductive. The guilt causes more stress which causes more guilt and . . .

So relax! Some stress is inevitable.

How Do You Cope?

Read the following list of statements and circle the numbers next to the ones that fit you in the past 12 months.

You've used illegal drugs. 100
You've felt depressed enough to think about suicide—
even if only briefly. 98
You've used prescription tranquilizers. 90
You've drunk enough alcohol to become intoxicated. 85
You've become violent in words or actions. 75
You smoke tobacco. 50
You're more than 20 pounds overweight. 45
You haven't exercised at least three times a week. 40
You haven't laughed out loud at least once a week. 35
You haven't let yourself cry. 30
You've worked at your job more than 50 hours a week. 30
You haven't had a hobby. 25
On average you've slept less than six hours a night. 20
You've gone shopping to relieve stress. 20
You haven't talked about your feelings to another adult
besides your spouse. 15
You haven't hugged often. 10

Total your score from the negative coping methods: _____

Write your score from the "Family Stress Test" on page 14 here: _____

Add the two scores together for your new total stress score: _____

Now evaluate your stress level based on the scoring evaluation on page 15. Does it change?

Assumption #2: Parents are people too. Always putting yourself last makes you a victim and builds resentment that can taint your relationship with your kids. You need to take care of yourself, just as you expect your kids to take care of themselves.

Assumption #3: It's a parent's job to be a parent. Sure we want our kids to like us, relate to us and eventually be our friends. But right now our job is to raise them. Just because they are big and almost look like adults doesn't mean they don't need a strong, firm, fair parent around.

Assumption #4: Placing limits on our kids won't turn them into murderers. It may make them angry. They may pout, throw tantrums and accuse you of being unfair. They may not speak to you for a couple of days. But as long as the limits are reasonable and communicated clearly, you'll all survive.

Assumption #5: The best way to deal with stress is to prevent it. Talking, reasoning, making deals, communicating, bargaining, negotiating—these are ways we deal constructively with unwanted stress in our families.

► *Learning to Cope*

Developing positive responses to stress will lessen its impact on us and our families. This book introduces you to—or helps you get reacquainted with—healthy ways to cope with the stress that is inevitable in families.

We'll look at stresses you'll encounter in parenting and family life, and we'll talk about specific ways you can respond without fighting or fleeing.

You won't learn how to make stress disappear. But you'll discover ways to make the trip down parenting lane a little less bumpy and a little more exhilarating.

CHAPTER 2

Must We Lose Our Effervescence When Our Kids Reach Adolescence?

Effervesce: to be lively or vivacious. From the Latin, *effervescere*, to boil over.

Parents usually can relate to the "boiling over" part. It's "being lively or vivacious" that escapes us.

Funny how one word can have both meanings.

Perhaps adolescence is like that too. Having a teenager in the family can bring us to our boiling points. But it can also make things lively and vivacious. How we cope with the special stress of having a teenager will determine whether we bubble or boil.

► Teenagers Under Stress

Think about stress. Bring to mind everything you know, have read and can remember about its causes and effects.

Now take that last part—the effects—and double it. Welcome to the world of teenage stress.

Adolescence is scary, dangerous and troublesome, and it affects the whole family. What's more, it's absolutely normal and healthy. It's part of what makes teenagers so exciting—so effervescent.

Most kids will—with adult help—work through stress to

become strong, healthy, productive adults. So while these things may be painful, their potential for positive growth can be amazing. Here's why.

Teenagers magnify the importance of events. I kiss my wife about 10 or 15 times a day. We hug regularly, hold hands, give neck and back rubs. We're touchers.

We don't even think about it very much. It's just part of our relationship—no big deal.

But it wasn't always like this.

We met when we were teenagers. My stomach still does flip-flops when I think about our first date. Should I try to hold her hand? kiss her? What's she thinking about me? Is she having a good time? Maybe we should have done something else. What?

It was a terrible, wonderful, frightening, exciting, magical evening. I thought I might die. I thought I had died and was in heaven . . . or hell. I didn't know which.

I was going out with the most beautiful girl in the world for the greatest date in my life, I told myself. But when I look back, I realize it was really a routine, teenage date. But it seemed like such a big event!

Teenagers tend to see life in its extremes. For them, life and death hang in the balance with basketball games, final exams, dates, cheerleader tryouts, play auditions, tests, and arguments with Mom and Dad.

Of course, life doesn't really depend on these day-to-day events. In a few years, they'll look back and realize most of these events were actually just a few of the many things that happen to most teenagers.

But for now, life and death are suspended by a thread.

And if the event is that important, then so is the success or failure that flows from the event. The success is the sweetest, most wonderful success. And the failure is the worst, most painful failure.

It's no wonder those events—which seem normal for adults—are highly stressful for teenagers.

Teenagers have limited self-determination. Barry, a teenager in our church, was telling the youth group how he lost the brakes on his old car while going down a hill toward a crowded intersection.

He panicked, forgot everything he learned in drivers education, and plowed into the back of a Volkswagen bug, totaling it. Several people were hurt, though none seriously. Barry was cited and taken to the police station.

One of the girls in our group began to pale as Barry told the story. And just as he got to the part about the police station, she interrupted with an almost involuntary gasp and said, "And you had to call your dad!"

The room grew deathly silent. Everyone looked at Barry. He nodded his head, then sadly shook it back and forth.

One car totaled, his car towed away, people hurt, a moving violation. But the saddest thing of all: He had to call his dad.

Few urges are stronger in teenagers than the drive for self-determination—to be independent and do things on their own. They crave it, need it, want it and strive for it constantly. God made them that way. Without the drive, they'd never mature.

While teenagers want to decide for themselves, make their own choices and be responsible for their actions, they're also afraid of the responsibilities that go along with it.

So parents become a mixed blessing for teenagers. On one hand, they'll bail you out when you get in trouble. On the other hand, parents make all the big decisions for you—where you'll live, what you'll eat and other choices. And teenagers often resent those decisions—even while they're thankful they didn't have to make the choices themselves.

Stress.

Teenagers struggle for a self-determination or independence that's dangerous, scary and exciting—all at the same time. They begin making decisions about money, relationships, God and their future. They're excited by the opportunity, but scared too.

Stress.

Teenagers experience rapid change. Imagine moving to a new department at work every year. Your colleagues would change, your boss would change, your job description would change, and the required knowledge and skills would change.

How long would you last in such a job? After about

Skills for Adulthood

Between the ages of 12 and 20 our kids must deal with some pretty tough stuff. They'll have to acquire important skills of adulthood. But that takes hard work and can cause lots of stress. By knowing what the skills are, you can provide the support they need. Here, briefly, are the major areas of growth and change:

Sexuality—Around age 12 our kids enter puberty. Whamo! Changes and stresses galore. Body hair, changing shapes and sizes, new feelings and thoughts, erections and wet dreams for boys, menstruation for girls. It's all pretty stressful stuff.

Achievement—Teenagers need to find out what they are good at, and do it. This is done primarily through trial and error. To find out where they can succeed, they will have to fail.

Friends—Kids need to learn how to make and keep friends. If they don't, they'll remain family dependent like small children. Instinctively, they know this. Friends are very important to them. But it's so scary. Rejection lurks around every corner.

Feelings—When kids say, "But you don't understand," they're probably right. After all, how can you understand if they never tell you? Part of growing up is learning to identify and articulate feelings. A poverty of feeling-words and the inability to talk about feelings can cause painful stress.

Identity—I'm Ben and Sarah's dad. I'm Jean's husband. I'm Donna and Marv's son. I'm Scot, Lisa, Brian and Ben's brother. But beyond those relationships, I'm Dean.

During our teenage years, we first begin to really grapple with our identities beyond the role we play in our families. The question, "Who am I?" is real and important for teenagers. And finding the answer can be as stressful as anything we do.

Responsibility—Teenagers—between the ages of 12 and 20—must learn to take responsibility for their actions. Good or bad. This responsibility business causes a lot of stress. On one hand, kids want to be treated like adults. But on the other hand, they want to find scapegoats to take the blame for their actions.

two years, your resume would no doubt be in the hands of every potential employer within 2,000 miles.

But that's exactly what happens to teenagers every year. Seventh grade, eighth grade, freshman, sophomore, junior, senior. With each new year come new teachers, new classmates, new skills, new requirements. While kids may look forward to the changes, the changes are extremely stressful.

At the same time, kids' bodies undergo rapid and extreme changes. Growth, sexual maturity, muscle development and skeletal changes come fast. It's not uncommon for a teenager to go from short and chubby in the spring of the eighth grade to tall and lanky in the fall of the ninth grade.

In the midst of the physical changes, teenagers fall in and out of love. They make and drop friends. They can't do things they used to be able to do. And they can suddenly do things they couldn't do just six months earlier.

One day they're not mature enough to drive. Then a magical day comes—their 16th birthday. And suddenly they're supposed to be responsible and trustworthy behind the steering wheel.

We've lived through all these changes and turned out okay. So we assume our kids will too. But we often forget the powerful stress the changes can cause.

Teenagers face compounded stress. Sixteen-year-old Anne sat beside me on an old picnic table and related this story.

She had been going with David for a whole year (stress). They had a fight (stress) . . . about sex (stress) . . . Now it looks like they may break up (stress) . . . but she isn't sure (stress) . . . The situation was left unresolved (stress).

Because of this fight she couldn't concentrate when she was studying for her American history exam (stress, stress) . . . So she got a D (stress) . . . The test paper is now in her purse, and has to be signed by her parents (stress)—who expect her to be a B student (stress).

She asked her friends (stress) what to do about David. Her friends, Alice and Bridgette, gave her conflicting advice (stress).

All of this stress has made her skin oily (stress) . . . And she now has an enormous zit (stress) . . . right between her eyes (stress) . . . Cheerleader tryouts are next week (stress) . . . and she's getting her period (stress).

At this point she burst into tears.

Whew! Where to start? Teenage stresses, magnified in importance as they are, build on each other. One stress causes another that causes another and another.

Teenagers are pushed into premature adulthood. I met Carrie Lynn a couple of years ago at an inner-city workcamp. She was tall for her age, thin and very driven. I suspected she'd go far.

She got straight A's in school—which was an accomplishment. Her mother was divorced and worked as a domestic worker at odd hours. Sometimes Carrie Lynn had to fix breakfast, and get herself and her sister Dottie dressed and off to school. After school she worked part time to supplement her mother's income.

Carrie Lynn hoped to become a doctor. She certainly was smart enough—and driven enough. I hope she made it. But I wonder.

When I knew her, Carrie Lynn was only 12 years old. She'd lied to get her job. If her boss found out, she'd have to get another.

As Carrie Lynn told me her story, she constantly scratched up and down, up and down her right forearm. I could see the scabs where she'd scratched it raw on some previous occasion. Carrie Lynn suffered from severe stress. Her nervous energy made her scratch herself. I call it the stress of premature adulthood.

Simply put, premature adulthood is having to act like an adult, make adult decisions, take on adult responsibilities, think like an adult, before you're ready. Granted, not every teenager is in Carrie Lynn's desperate situation. But most teenagers today experience much of the same stress she faced.

Some of these stresses, kids bring on themselves. Some are placed on them by our culture. Let's look at some common causes:

- Jobs—Kids want jobs. Our culture admires kids who have jobs—who pay their own way. Kids like the money

"I don't understand why you don't want to go to the dinner party next week. Think of all the potential employers you could meet!"

and freedom a job represents. Parents like the break from having to provide every cent of a teenager's spending money.

But with a job comes stress. Most jobs throw teenagers in with adults—where they're expected to think, act and get along in an adult setting. Learning, thinking, maturing aren't on the agenda at work—making money is. Tomorrow's history test is of little consequence to most bosses.

● Sibling care—Babysitting is a great way for teenagers to make money. But teenagers aren't good parents. Expecting them to act like parents by taking care of younger children—for hours on end, day in and day out—is expecting them to be premature adults. The stress can be unbearable. Sooner or later they either make a bad mistake or collapse from the stress.

● Too much to do—Cramming everything that needs doing into a tight schedule is an activity best left to adults. Kids need to play, to relax, to be spontaneous. Often, they don't have time for all the activities, programs, clubs and organizations adults have created for them.

But kids try to be involved. We want them to, encourage them to and push them to. So they become all business—premature adults. No wonder they're stressed.

● College and career worries—I know a girl who spent 10 weekends of her senior year visiting colleges.

I know a seventh-grader who has already taken a college entrance test—twice . . . just for practice!

I know a high school freshman who's taking a summer course in college-level math so he can get a head start on other kids who want to be engineers.

I know a high school junior who can't sleep at night because she doesn't know whether to go to her mother's or father's alma mater.

Is this healthy? Does this kind of stress help our kids? Must our kids start dealing with career stress when they are 12 or 13 years old? Are they ready yet?

A brief look at the drug abuse statistics, suicide rates, alcohol consumption figures and police reports on high-achieving teenagers gives us reason to believe this stress hurts our kids.

● Information overload—Our kids are bombarded by

information. Television, school, movies, radio, books, magazines, newspapers—all are bringing more and more information faster than ever before.

This bountiful information wouldn't be a problem if kids had time to sort it out, digest it and use it as they needed. But with jobs, activities, families, sweethearts, churches, school work, college and career worries—and just trying to keep up—it just keeps building and building. Kids can't handle or process it. So they worry about it.

Teenagers often have poor coping techniques. As stressful as the teenage years are, you'd think kids would develop great coping techniques. But, sadly, they usually don't.

Instead of learning to deal with or escape from stressful situations, they try to escape from the symptoms of stress.

Instead of preparing for a potentially stressful situation, they bury themselves in music or fantasies so they won't think about their problems.

Instead of asking for a supportive, affectionate hug from a parent or friend, they seek physical affection in sexual intimacy with a sweetheart.

Instead of dealing head-on with the cause of their stress, they escape into another activity or event, piling activity upon activity—which only adds more stress.

Instead of seeking parental or adult help, they seek peer approval in the vain hope that such approval will ease the tension in their lives. Unfortunately, that longing for peer approval often causes the greatest stress.

Tragically, instead of expressing their feelings and frustrations, kids sometimes try to dull the pains of stress with drugs or alcohol.

Spend just a few minutes with teenagers, and you'll see them trying to eat stress away, sweat it away, talk it away, kiss it away, drown it out with music, ignore it, hide from it, argue with it and crowd it out of their lives.

But most of these techniques don't work. And they usually cause more stress. Catch-22.

What About Your Teenager?

For each of the statements about teenagers in the left column, list two or three events from your teenager's experience. Then think of ways—positive and negative—you and your teenager respond to that stress.

If you don't see this stress in your teenager, list your reasons and possible explanation across the last three columns.

Stress	Illustrations
Teenagers magnify the importance of events.	
Teenagers have limited self-determination.	
Teenagers experience rapid change.	
Teenagers face compounded stress.	
Teenagers are pushed into premature adulthood.	
Teenagers often have poor coping techniques.	

Your Responses	Your Teenager's Responses

► *Families Under Stress*

Remember Anne, the 16-year-old whose life seemed unbearable because of compounded stress? In the midst of her stress over David, American history and everything else, she can't understand why her parents aren't more understanding and supportive.

Anne realizes she sometimes doesn't handle stress well, but why can't they lighten up? Why can't they give her a little space? back off? let her deal with it in her own way without hassling her all the time? Why can't they remember how it was when they were kids? Why can't they see things from her viewpoint?

Anne doesn't realize she's asking the impossible. Parents who've lovingly watched a child's every move for 12 years don't suddenly "back off" because their child becomes a teenager.

The fact is, her parents do remember their teenage years very well indeed. And that's why they're hanging closer than ever to Anne. When Anne reached adolescence, so did the whole family. And with her, the whole family has encountered new and unique stresses.

Teenage stresses are family stresses. A teenager under stress means a family under stress. There's a certain "yours, mine, ours"-ness about teenage stress.

It won't be long before Anne's stresses finally blow up in the family. The American history exam will probably detonate a much larger explosion than anyone in the family expects.

Already feeling defensive and guilty, she'll present the test to her parents. A parental response will be spoken about the test. But it won't be Anne-of-the-D-on-the-test who hears it. It'll be Anne-of-the-D-on-the-test-of-the-fight-with-David-of-the-conflicting-friends-of-the-zit-on-the-forehead-and-of-the-cheerleader-tryouts who will hear it. And it'll be this Anne who responds—probably in a loud voice.

A fight will erupt, Mom and Dad will be upset, siblings will be caught in the middle, dinner will be ruined, the dog will get kicked and chaos will reign.

As a parent I may have job stress. But it's largely *my*

stress, and I try to keep it in perspective. I know it comes with the territory of my chosen career. With a few exceptions I find ways to deal with it that don't include dumping it on my family. In fact, my family is often my most effective escape from stress. That's where I get my hugs, my praise, my gentle words, my renewed self-esteem, my reassurance—my warm fuzzies.

But because of an event's magnified importance, limited self-determination and poor coping techniques, teenagers tend to dump their stress on the family instead of escaping from it in the family. Their stress becomes the family's stress.

Parents have unmet expectations. Face it, we all have expectations for our kids. We want them to be successful, happy, creative, kind, gentle, responsible, respectful, cheerful, thrifty, brave, clean and reverent.

When they aren't—when they don't meet our expectations—we're disappointed. And often angry.

Because teenagers are striving for self-determination, they seem to have an uncanny way of finding out our expectations and going in the exact opposite direction.

We call it rebellion or ingratitude or any number of things (mostly negative). And we take kids' responses as personal attacks on us and our values. We forget that the pain we feel is usually unintended and part of natural growth and maturation.

But even if we remember the reasons for the response and handle it with grace and dignity, it still causes stress.

Family relationships can change suddenly. Not long ago I gave a speech to parents, teachers and teenagers at a local high school. I talked about the changes that take place in the parent-child relationship after adolescence begins.

After the speech I was drinking punch and visiting with members of the audience when a father—with glistening eyes and a sad smile on his face—came up to me. As he shook my hand, he also shook his head. "What ever happened to my little princess?" he asked.

I wanted to cry with him. I, too, have a little princess. Right now she's seven years old, and I'm her pride and joy. As we walk down the street, hand in hand, it's all she can do to keep from telling perfect strangers, "This is my dad!"

What About Your Family?

Answer the following questions about how having a teenager affects the stress level in your family.

1. What evidence do you see in your family that teenage stresses are family stresses?

2. How does the stress your teenager feels affect your family life?

3. What unmet expectations do you have for your kids?

4. What happens when your kids don't live up to those expectations?

5. How have you seen your relationship change with your teenager? Describe the relationship as you remember it at the different stages:

- Ages 1 to 2:
- Ages 3 to 4:
- Ages 5 to 7:
- Ages 8 to 10:
- Ages 11 to 14:
- Ages 15 to 17:

6. What worries you most about the changes you see—and foresee—in your teenager?

7. What excites you the most about the changes?

She wants to be a minister when she grows up—"like my daddy." At school, she writes me notes that she puts on my pillow when she gets home.

I love it.

But I also know that while this is a wonderful, healthy, beautiful relationship for a father and a seven-year-old daughter, something would be wrong if our relationship were the same when she's 16.

In her teenage years she'll be establishing her identity beyond her relationship with her daddy. She'll begin becoming independent. She'll begin breaking away from me.

It'll be painful for both of us. We'll argue and disagree and probably fight. Rules will be established and broken. And discipline will be imposed. No longer will I be "Daddy" and she "Princess." I'll be "Dad" and she'll be "Sarah."

The stress will be painful. Sometimes it'll seem unbearable. Occasionally—for a few moments—we'll both give in and tumble back into our old ways of Daddy and Princess once again.

But we'll not dare stay there long, because something in each of us will know that the change, the stress, the pain we're experiencing is the stress and pain of birth. Through it all, I'll be able to see a new Sarah—an independent, determined, capable, adult Sarah—emerging into the world.

And each time I take time to notice this new Sarah—be it briefly or for long periods of time—I'll lift my eyes to heaven and thank God for this wonderful miracle called adolescence. And I'll ask for the strength and tools to help me cope with the inevitable stress that comes with it.

CHAPTER 3

The Business of Busyness

When people think of stress, they immediately talk about all the things they have to do. And for most families these days, schedule conflicts and time problems cause a lot of stress.

Here's a test you can take to see how big the time problem is for you and your family. For each statement, circle the appropriate number.

Time Flies

	Rarely						Usually
1. In my family, my time is not my own.	1	2	3	4	5	6	7
2. My kids usually set the schedule, and I have to fit in where I can.	1	2	3	4	5	6	7
3. I feel like I have to make an appointment to use my own telephone.	1	2	3	4	5	6	7
4. Basically, my kids think of me as a chauffeur, cleaning service and social secretary.	1	2	3	4	5	6	7
5. Vacations and holidays are planned around the kids' schedules.	1	2	3	4	5	6	7

6. Our family rarely eats a meal together.	1	2	3	4	5	6	7
7. I feel like I have to ask my kids' permission before I can go out for an evening.	1	2	3	4	5	6	7
8. Sunday morning causes more stress than any other morning in our house.	1	2	3	4	5	6	7
9. My teenager and I regularly fight or argue about car use.	1	2	3	4	5	6	7
10. I feel guilty about not spending enough time with my kids.	1	2	3	4	5	6	7
11. My job keeps me from being the kind of parent I ought to be.	1	2	3	4	5	6	7
12. I have more than two responsibilities at church.	1	2	3	4	5	6	7
13. I can't seem to get caught up on housework.	1	2	3	4	5	6	7
14. I bring my work home with me more than once a week.	1	2	3	4	5	6	7
15. My job calls for me to be away from home overnight.	1	2	3	4	5	6	7

Now total your score and see where you stand: ________

If you scored 10 to 30—Are you for real? If things are going this well, skip this chapter and move on. You may also want to consider getting an agent. Your family is the stuff TV shows are made of.

If you scored 31 to 45—Whatever you're doing, it's working for you. Don't fix what isn't broken, but read this chapter anyway. You might find ways to shore up the few weak points in your system.

If you scored 46 to 75—You're pretty normal. As we said, time and schedule conflicts cause stress—and you're having your share. Things haven't reached a crisis, but they could if you aren't careful. Read on and head off trouble before it comes your way.

If you scored 76 to 105—Crisis time! Your time-stress is consuming you. Take immediate and decisive steps. This chapter is dedicated to you.

► *Making Time*

If you could buy time, how much would you buy? What would you use it for? How much would you pay for it?

Regardless of how you answer those questions, you'll never have more than 24 hours a day, seven days a week and 52 weeks a year. Everyone has the same amount of time. What's different is how you use the time you have.

The problem is that it's easy to fill up whatever time you have available. Responsibilities tend to take as much time as you give them. So unless you intentionally claim time in the schedule for your family, you'll never find it.

The best way to claim time for what's important is to set priorities, guidelines and limits. This approach not only helps you manage your own schedule, but it helps teenagers understand what's expected. You'll discover that family life isn't so rushed and stressed.

Launch your attack with these ideas.

Set time priorities and hold to them. When I was a teenager, my family had three time priorities that were inviolable. We went to church together on Sunday morning. We ate dinner together after church. And we went on vacation together.

No excuses. Out late on a date Saturday night? Too bad. You knew the rule when you stayed out late. Getting a summer job? Great! Just make sure your boss knows you'll be gone the first two weeks in August.

Granted, my parents didn't just lay down the rules.

They helped us abide by them when they could. They made suggestions and helped us get summer jobs we could be away from for vacation. We often ate Sunday dinner at a restaurant—sometimes even fast-food. And we usually went to the late service on Sunday morning so we could sleep in—if only a little.

But we all knew the priorities and what was expected.

To get a similar process started, talk to your kids about what things you consider priorities for family time. Use "I" statements to explain your needs and expectations. Then ask your kids what they'd add to the list. Negotiate and compromise if necessary. But be firm.

If going to church as a family is a priority for you, say so. "I want to worship with my family on Sundays." But be sensitive to other people's needs as well. "I'm willing to go to an earlier service so you can have most of the day for your activities."

Plan ahead. Flexibility is nice in a family. But it can't be the underlying principle for everything you do. If you try to make it so, you end up with confusion.

When flexibility becomes a style, kids don't know what to expect. It's okay to drive the car today, but not tomorrow. It's okay to spend the afternoon with your friends this week, but it may not be okay next week . . . or it may be. You never know. It depends.

On what?

On how someone feels. On what comes up. On who calls. On biorhythms, for all I know.

Flexibility is a gift to give your kids in the context of consistency. It says, "Usually, we do things this way, but this time we'll make an exception." Create the overall context of consistency by planning ahead.

Around our house, Advent is the most hectic time of the year. So I make a big calendar and hang it on the basement door. The family car, the family house, the family money and energy are all subject to that calendar. First come, first served.

Following the calendar isn't easy for anyone, but it sure prevents a lot of fights. A couple of times I've been frozen out of something. What a neat experience for my kids to hear me say no to something I wanted to do because the family schedule wouldn't allow it! They realize they aren't the only ones who don't get everything they want.

Occasionally I assert my parental authority when I X out several days for "family discontinuity." This is time when we all plan to do nothing—and do it together. It's one of our priorities.

Use this model when planning vacations, weekends away and days off together. Get those events on the calendar early—in red. That says: This is a priority time. Don't mess with it.

Set limits on involvement. All of us get too busy from time to time. Parents get caught up in job overload, community activities, church responsibilities, volunteer work and any number of other responsibilities. Kids spend their time on school, homework, part-time jobs, youth group, extracurricular activities, athletics or any of many other opportunities.

By themselves, each of these activities may be healthy, useful and important. But they quickly snowball out of control. A church task force that "won't take much time" turns into a weekly headache. A teenager's bit part in the play takes up three or four nights every week. One activity builds on another until none of the "opportunities" are enjoyable.

Part of acting like a "we" involves setting limits on involvement so you can spend time together as a family—and so family members don't become so crabby they can't enjoy each other.

The next time someone in the family wants to take on another commitment or get involved in another project or event, have him or her take "The Busy Test" on page 41.

Of course, just when you resolve not to take on another job, the telephone rings: "We've just formed this committee to address this vital problem in our community. We want it to include just the right people. And you're perfect for the job . . . It'll only take a few hours . . . Will you do it?"

That's when it's critical to know how to say no. Consult the family schedule before you take on a new commitment. When you have to say no, say it firmly and with authority.

Finding a positive way to decline makes you and the

The Busy Test

Check all the questions you say yes to.

- ☐ Have you eaten fewer than three meals with your family in the past week?
- ☐ Do you have trouble getting to sleep or do you feel tired all the time?
- ☐ Do you spend less than two hours a day, on average, doing something just for the fun of it?
- ☐ Do you spend more than two hours a day, on average, working on stuff you'd rather not do?
- ☐ Have you missed more than three important family occasions in the past month?
- ☐ Did you read fewer than three books for pleasure in the last year?
- ☐ Do you find you're still tired two hours after you get out of bed?
- ☐ Have you spent less than 90 minutes talking to members of your family in the past week?
- ☐ In the past month, have you taken on a commitment that, later, you wished you didn't have to do?
- ☐ Are you more short-tempered than usual?

If you checked more than three questions, you're probably too busy to take on another commitment. Just say no.

person who's asking feel better. Instead of saying, "No, I'm sorry, I just can't," say: "I'm flattered to be asked. But I'm afraid I can't right now. Our family schedule is already full, and my getting involved would take away important time from my family."

Remember, your ministry to and through your family is just as important as any other ministry you undertake. We serve the Lord faithfully when we budget our time to include our families as well as work, church and community service.

Use similar criteria when limiting your teenagers' involvement. Learn to say no to your kids when they haven't learned to say no themselves. Use the family schedule as your reason.

"I know you'd like to sing in the school swing choir. But you're already a cheerleader, a band member and the lead in the spring play. The family schedule just can't handle any more. For you to do this will mean that you—or someone else—will have to give up something."

This approach to dealing with your kids makes more sense and is less painful to hear than: "No, you can't take on any more. You'll kill yourself—and me along with you."

In some cases, a fallback position may be appropriate. "You may join the choir as long as your grades aren't affected and you keep the commitments you've already made."

Let values determine the schedule. You want to do one thing, and your son wants to do another. You argue. You fight. You're tempted to fall back on parental authority and make a ruling.

Stop!

Before you make that ruling, consider what values are at work. Ask yourself:

- Will the ruling be determined by convenience, desires, wants, wishes or anger? Or by other, more important things?
- Are you ruling because it's your policy? Fine, but ask yourself why that's the policy. If you don't, your teenager will.

Those questions lead to questions about priorities. Is it really so important to get the house cleaned? Or could the time be better spent fishing? Is it really necessary to go to the office on Saturday? Or would the family be better served by doing yard work together?

When we clarify what's valuable—what's most important—sometimes the time questions are easier to answer.

Operate as "we," not "me and them." This principle is one that's easy to forget. Wills get asserted. Power becomes an issue. Fights begin. And family life becomes a struggle for control—of the car, the schedule, the money or whatever else is involved.

The family schedule is *our* schedule, not my schedule and your schedule. When a conflict arises, "we have a conflict." It isn't "you're conflicting with me."

When I was 18, one of my best friends fought constantly with his parents about going out with his friends. They wanted to know where he was going, who he'd be with and when he'd come home. He resented their desire to keep tabs on him.

One night my friend's mother called me. His father had suffered a heart attack. Would I send her son home immediately?

I would have, but he wasn't with me.

He wasn't? Where was he?

I didn't know.

We began the search. I called all our mutual friends to try to find him. They called others. It took us four hours to find him. By then it was too late. His father died on the way to the hospital.

That was the first time I truly realized my parents weren't keeping tabs on me just trying to control me. They wanted to know where I was and when I'd be back because they needed me. And they wanted me to keep tabs on them. If my friend had realized that, he might have been able to say good-bye to his father.

Operating as a "we" lets us keep tabs on those we love.

We teach our kids to operate as a "we" by offering them the same courtesies we expect. It's simple to tell a teenager: "I'll be at the Smith's until about 9, then I'll stop at the grocery store on my way home. So you can expect me around 10."

Let your own behavior exhibit "we" values. Be on time. Keep promises and commitments. If there's a problem or you're going to be late, call. Don't drink and drive.

In other words, do all the things we ask of our kids. If we encourage them to keep tabs on us, they'll be a lot more tolerant of our keeping tabs on them.

Offer and expect reciprocity in free time. It works like this: "Yes, you may use the car to go out on Friday night. And your father and I are using it to go out on Saturday night."

Favors are exchanged for favors. Courtesies for courtesies. Freedoms for freedoms. We all get a little of what we want.

► *Handling Time Stresses*

General guidelines about managing time are fine. But what about all the day-to-day squabbles? That's where we feel the stress. The telephone, television, car,—these are the things we fight about. Let's talk about how to handle the stress that occurs when one person's needs clash with someone else's.

Kids' overactivity—Kids are busy these days. No doubt you've noticed. Band, choir, drama, sports, church choir, youth group events. Everyone wants our kids to be active.

And because our *kids* are active, *we're* active. The drama group needs a costume maker or a stage manager. The band needs parents to be boosters. The baseball team needs an equipment manager.

And everyone wants an audience.

So we're expected to encourage our kids to participate, take them to practice, help prepare for the event, raise money to support the organization *and* pay for tickets so we can watch.

And what's worse, a little voice inside our brains keeps saying, "you ought . . . you should . . . you ought . . ." Talk about stress! It's easier for the kids. All they have to do is show up, practice and perform!

Talking with our kids about this concern early and often helps us deal with expectations and fantasies before someone is disappointed. And the more we prevent disappointment, anger and frustration, the more we prevent stress.

Set down the conditions under which you'll participate in your teenager's activities. Let him or her know what to expect from you. Be specific. And don't feel you have to do something just because your child asks. (You can say no to a teenager too.) Participate in activities you enjoy.

My kids know my talents lie in theater, music and print. I'm interested in sports, but I'm not much of a jock. If they need someone with carpentry skills to help build a set for their play, they know I'm their man.

If they need an assistant coach for "a couple of days a week sometime this spring," I probably won't be available. Most likely, I'll be doing something I find more enjoyable . . . like drinking molten lead.

If your teenager really wants you to be present for a certain event, make sure it gets on the family schedule early. Then treat it as you would treat other important events. Honor it and make time for it.

The telephone—To say teenagers like to talk on the phone is an understatement. They *love* to talk on the phone. Sometimes it seems that's all they do from the minute they step in the door to the instant they rush out to be with their friends.

Teenagers' phone use might not be a stress in the family if other people didn't want—or need—to use the phone too. But they do. So teenagers using the phone often becomes a major source of tension in families.

This suggestion may get me into trouble with some people but I'm going to make it anyway: If there's any way you can swing it, get your teenager his or her own phone line.

The telephone isn't just a toy for teenagers. It's an invaluable tool in their development. Part of growing up involves learning to identify, articulate and communicate feelings. And the telephone provides a safe, non-confrontive way to learn these skills. Kids can talk about their feelings without having to look someone in the eye.

If you can't get a separate line, get your teenager his or her own phone.

"This'll get their attention!"

If you have a single phone line in your home, create a phone schedule. For example, give your teenager free use of the phone from, say, 7 to 9 p.m. and from 11 p.m. to midnight. Between 9 and 11 p.m., the phone is to be left free for others to use—whether they're talking on it or not. Such a schedule won't be easy for anyone. But most of the time you can schedule calls within such a framework. And a call-waiting feature will keep you from missing a call while your teenager is on the phone.

The television—I'm not as hard on television as many people. I like it, and I like to watch it with my kids . . . sometimes. It certainly provides a mindless escape—something we all need occasionally.

But it can also eat up precious family time. When families never interact—except to argue about which channel to watch—and spend all family time in a vegetative state in front of the tube, the escape idea seems farfetched.

The trick, then, is not to let your kids—or yourself—escape too much or too often. Set limits. Plan your TV viewing. Circle the programs you expect to watch in the TV guide. Make the schedule a family decision.

The same principle holds true with the VCR. Plan what movies you're going to watch, and invite your kids to watch them with you. Sharing a favorite movie and talking about it can be a neat experience.

Eventually your teenager may want his or her own television. My experience is that if the teenager helps pay for it, it's probably okay. The teenager will watch it a lot for the first month. Then it'll become just another dust collector in their room.

Seek out alternatives to television. We tend to forget about them when our kids get older. Try these:

- Read to each other.
- Listen to a radio drama together.
- Play Scrabble or other board games.
- Go for a family walk.
- Work together on a school or church project.
- Make a tape of your own radio drama.
- Work around the house together.
- Play a game of catch.

These kinds of alternatives may fill the same need for relaxation and entertainment that we expect from television. But they're far more constructive and give us more chances to interact as a family.

When my kids were little, I learned that I hated kiddie games—Chutes and Ladders, Uncle Wiggiley . . . you know the ones. But I wanted to do stuff with my kids. Then I discovered—much to my pleasure—that my kids really liked doing adult stuff with me.

So we washed the car, weeded the garden, baked pies, raked leaves and did all kinds of adult things together. The tasks took longer. But we got to enjoy each other's company while we did them.

You don't have to spend a fortune entertaining your kids. Just be with them.

The car—Learning to drive a car is an important rite of passage for most American teenagers. When a teenager reaches that point, some parents feel as though they'll never drive their car again. Andy or Margaret always has it.

To avoid stress and conflict when a teenager starts driving, plan ahead. Set limits before your teenager gets his or her driver's license. This way you'll pre-empt any fantasies or false expectations about car use, and you won't have to deal with them later.

Address and discuss these things before your teenager starts asking for the car keys:

- Driving is a privilege, not a right. Your teenager has to earn the use of the car.
- Driving a car is expensive. Who'll pay for its use?
- Driving a car requires sound judgment and snap decisions. Evidence of these two in other areas will make you feel better about letting your teenager drive the car.
- A car is a huge, dangerous machine—not a toy. It must be handled with respect and care. If your teenager shows respect and care in other areas, you'll more likely trust him or her behind the wheel of a car.
- In most cases, the car belongs to you. You earned it and did without to get it. Your teenager uses it at your pleasure. A little good will on the part of your teenager will go a long way in garnering this pleasure from you.

● When determining whether to let your teenager use the car, talk with your teenager about who'll provide transportation if he or she doesn't. My parents often found that they rested easier knowing I was driving—not one of my friends, who they knew little about.

Missed mealtimes—Mealtimes can be important times for family interaction—a chance to "touch base" for a few relaxed minutes. But for many people, family meals are anomalies reserved for Thanksgiving, Christmas and Easter.

Through the rest of the year, each family member is scurrying in a different direction, heating something quick in the microwave or going through a drive-through window to pick up something to eat at traffic lights.

Help build your family and slow down for a while each day by making family meals a priority several times each week. Establish family meals in advance and—within certain flexible limits—expect everyone to be present.

Then when you're together, make it a positive time for everyone. Try these suggestions:

● Use the setting to set the right mood. If family fights take place in the kitchen, eat in the dining room. Or go out.

In my family we've established what we call the living room picnic for special meals. We do this when the living room is our only alternative to a crowded, messy kitchen. And it's a fun change when outside picnics aren't practical. Be sure the television stays off.

● Don't use mealtimes to solve problems. Set up a problem-solving time to do that. Use meals together for sharing feelings, ideas, insights and experiences. Talk and listen to each other.

● Talk about anything! What's the best movie of all time? Why do you think so? Who was the greatest football player of all time? If you had to choose between being rich or famous, which would you choose? What's the best novel you've ever read? What's the best thing on television? the worst?

Questions like these can bring back memories and ideas that open up everyone's desire to share. A great source for questions to ask in families is *Talk Triggers* by Thom and Joani Schultz (Group Books).

Bathrooms—Bathroom stress comes from two basic sources: people who never clean up after themselves and too many people wanting to use a bathroom at the same time.

My mother had a unique way of solving the first problem, and I recommend it highly. When you find a mess in the bathroom, pick it up and put it on the bed of the person who left it. Wet towels, toothbrush, bath sponge, shower cap, razor, whatever—on the bed it goes. I guarantee your bathroom will be nice and tidy before very long.

Warning: Make sure you clean up your own messes. Kids love nothing better than to turn the tables on you. It was no fun sleeping on the spot where they threw my wet towel.

If your family has the second type of stress, another bathroom isn't your only solution. Try these two steps:

- Step 1—Only use the bathroom for things that must be done in a bathroom. Virtually everything that doesn't require running water can be done elsewhere.

A well-lighted mirror and a small table in another room or a niche in the hallway can serve as a makeup area. An electric razor can get you out of the bathroom and is cheaper in the long run.

Absolutely forbid certain activities in the bathroom. These include: reading, listening to the radio, talking on the telephone, admiring yourself in the mirror, pouting, wrapping Christmas presents, washing clothing. All of these can be accomplished just as easily in another room.

- Step 2—Establish a schedule. Give everyone in the family a certain time period for personal hygiene. These time periods can be violated only for, uh . . . emergencies.

Times not assigned to a specific person are available on a first-come, first-served basis. Common courtesy and Christian charity should govern these times.

Personal time and space—The need to be alone, to be quiet, to think without interruption or distraction is important for everyone. Researchers have even found that teenagers who have adequate privacy tend to be healthier—emotionally and physically.

But, sometimes privacy is hard to find in a family. I

What's Causing Time Stress?

As a family, evaluate what time problems cause the most stress in your family. Rank the specific areas discussed in this chapter (1=most stress; 7=least stress). If you need to, make two lists—one ranking parent stress and one ranking kid stress.

________ Kids' overactivity

________ The telephone

________ The television

________ The car

________ Missed mealtimes

________ Bathrooms

________ Personal time and space

________ Job pressures

Discuss:

- Why are the biggest stresses a problem in our family? (Get everyone's input.)

- What would we like to see happen regarding stress?

- What are some ways we might be able to deal with stress? (List all ideas on paper without judging.)

- What option might work best for our family?

- How and when can we begin dealing with the problem? (Set specific actions and deadlines.)

grew up sharing a bedroom with at least one sibling, sometimes more. Families who live in small houses, mobile homes and apartments will often have special stresses caused simply by crowding.

The antidote to this kind of stress is easier to prescribe than to administer. It requires selflessness and the ability to sacrifice for each other. Learn to do these things as a family:

● Communicate the need. Let people know you need quiet time by yourself. Make it clear that everyone in the family has the right to privacy.

● When you need to be alone, leave the room where everyone else is. It's unfair to expect everyone else to vacate a space just because you want it. Sometimes you may have to leave the house.

I found it was easier to be alone in a booth at a crowded local diner than in my own house. Some people go outside and mow grass, pull weeds or pick vegetables by themselves. Find ways that fit you.

● Come back. We all need to be alone from time to time. But enough is enough. If you find you simply can't stand being with your family for long—or if you detect this attitude in your teenager—it might be time to see a counselor.

● Handle personal space in a similar way. Make it clear there are two kinds of space in a family home—personal and family space. Personal space is private and inviolable, whether it's a whole room or a single dresser drawer. It's not to be intruded upon without permission—by anyone.

Job pressures—Sometimes your job can put time pressures on you that seem to be beyond your control. But time pressures on you often translate into time pressures on the whole family. What can you do about it?

If your job is taking family time away by adding overtime in the evenings, try getting up a little earlier in the morning. Have a hearty breakfast with the family. Have an early morning jog or walk the dog with your kids. Or do your extra work in the early morning time and save the evening for your family.

Some jobs have seasonal swings: lots of overtime in the spring and fall; downtimes in the summer and winter. If this is the case, plan family outings when the pressure is off.

If the extra hours you are putting in mean extra pay, use some of that pay to reward yourself and the family for enduring the time problems it caused. When I'm writing a book, my kids call it a "Christmas book" or a "vacation book." Knowing that dad is earning Christmas or vacation money makes it easier to do without him while he sits at the computer.

Finally, longer work hours may come from a promotion or a change in job description. Usually, we want these things. But remember, giving more time to work means taking it *away* from something else. Before you accept that promotion, ask yourself where the time for it will come from and if that time is really yours to give. Talk about it with your family to see how others feel.

► *Finding Solutions*

A couple of years ago, my whole family was just too busy. In addition to all the regular stuff, both kids were involved in soccer—which meant two games each on the weekends and at least one soccer practice each during the week. Jean was heavily involved in church and school, and I was working at church and writing and trying to go to all the kids' games.

One Saturday, Ben's soccer game ended and I headed for the car with my lawn chair. I was in a hurry—Sarah's game would end soon at a field several miles away, and we had to get over there to pick up her and Mom.

Ben piled into the car, sweating and beaming. "Well?" he queried before I'd closed my door.

"Well, what?" I said, smiling benignly back at him.

His face fell. "You didn't see it, did you?"

"Sure . . . see what?"

His face was blank now. His voice barely audible. "I made a goal."

I missed the only goal he made all year.

I'd taken my briefcase with me so I could catch up on some work during the game. I worked right through his goal and all the cheering that went with it. I felt awful.

That night we had a family meeting. I apologized to

Ben, and we took a close look at the family schedule. It was time to make some changes.

I'd limit my writing time to evenings. But I'd attend only one soccer game for each child each week. That way I could really watch the games I went to.

It was a small compromise for each of us, but it worked. I didn't have to be everywhere and do everything. But when I was there I was really there.

It wasn't perfect. But it worked.

As you deal with the time stresses in your family, you won't find perfect solutions. Everyone will have to compromise. No one will get to do everything he or she wants to do. But you can work it out so everyone's needs are met.

It won't be perfect. But it will work.

CHAPTER 4

Money Matters . . . But How Much?

A few weeks ago I was sitting in the food court at a mall, eating a frozen yogurt and reading a novel when I witnessed the following scene.

Dad was exhausted. He dropped his bags on a table and collapsed into a chair. Mom and the girls (about 12 and 14) weren't even winded.

"Okay, you get a cup of coffee and take a break. We'll just go look in that store that's having a sale," Mom said as she led the girls away.

Dad was grateful for the reprieve. He looked at me pleadingly, and I agreed to watch his things while he got his well-earned cup of coffee.

The coffee cup was still half full when Mom and the girls returned. Mom was red in the face, jaw clenched tightly. Older Sister was in a snit that threatened to explode into a tantrum. And Younger Sister had screwed up her face into the most awful pout you've ever seen. Before Mom could speak, both girls simultaneously yanked out chairs, flounced down in them and crossed their arms and legs at the same time. They stared into middle space.

The battle lines were drawn.

I pretended to read my novel as I watched.

"What?" asked Dad.

"Your daughters . . ."

Both girls uncrossed their legs and crossed them the

other way.

". . . don't understand the first thing about money," Mom said.

"What about it, girls?" Dad asked, trying to be diplomatic.

But it didn't work. Pandemonium ensued. Arguments, pleading, tears, threats, guilt, accusations, counteraccusations. It wasn't pretty.

●

Families argue about money more than anything else. While researching her book *Stress and the Healthy Family*, Dolores Curran discovered that 58 percent of married men, 66 percent of married women and 87 percent of single mothers consider finances to be one of the most significant stresses on their families.[1]

When Better Homes and Gardens surveyed 30,000 parents, 48 percent said finances cause the most difficulty in their families.[2]

Families never seem to have enough money. Mortgage or rent payments, ever-increasing utility rates, automobile payments, insurance, medical expenses, taxes, savings for college and retirement. The expenses make a comedy of our attempts to live within a budget.

Bringing teenagers into the family adds even more twists. Parents are often shocked to see grocery bills nearly double when their kids enter adolescence. Teenagers suddenly become style conscious. There's always something else out there they "just have to have." Everyone else's kids seem to have all the things our kids don't have . . . or at least that's what our kids tell us.

So more problems arise:

- Should we let them take a part-time job?
- Can we learn to talk about money without fighting about it?
- And what about charity? How can we be generous and kind to those who are less fortunate than ourselves when we never seem to have enough for our own necessities?

We're uncomfortable when we read that Jesus criticized the Pharisees for giving out of their excess and praised the widow who gave all she had (Luke 21:1-4). We realize we aren't judged by how much we give but by how much we keep for ourselves. And yet, what we keep for ourselves never seems to be enough. So what do we do?

► Money Mania

In Monopoly you get a financial reward just for surviving. Roll the dice, bypass "Income Tax," avoid the properties with high rent, stay out of jail and hotels on "Park Place," and what do you know . . . $200.

Would that it were so in real life.

In real life, getting, spending and keeping money can be a complicated task. Several attitudes and perceptions can push families toward financial stress.

Enough is never enough. Our culture tells us more is always better. New is better than old. Whatever you have can and should be improved.

No matter what kind of car you own, there's a better, faster, nicer one you could have for just a few more dollars.

No matter how sufficient your apartment, a bigger one would be better. And a house would be best of all. Or maybe a bigger house in a nicer part of town.

If you wash your clothes at a laundromat, you should be washing them at home. And if you wash them at home you should be washing them in a better, bigger, faster, smarter washing machine.

When a rich man was asked how much money was enough, he answered, "A little more." You don't have to be rich to know what he meant. It's hard to be satisfied with what we have.

You are what you own. As a culture, we often gauge our value as human beings by how much money we make and how much we can buy. We seem to say those who have much are doing something right . . . and those who have little are doing something wrong.

This attitude invades even our homes. Women who stay home to be mothers and homemakers tend, unfortunately, to see their contribution to the family as less valuable than their husband's. In families with more than one income, the person who makes the most money tends to have the most power in family decisions.

We have the same problem James confronted in the early church when the church gave preference to members who came "with gold rings and in fine clothing" (James 2:1-4).

Never discuss finances. Generally, families don't talk about money; they fight about it. And arguments rarely center on how much money is available. Rather they revolve around how to spend what money *is* available.

She wants to pay bills. He wants a new couch. The kids want a compact disc player. All gather their arguments and join the battle.

Usually, the person with the most money power—the one who makes the most money—wins. "When you start paying the bills around here, then you can make the decisions about . . ."

How many times have we heard statements like that?

How many times have we said them?

Eventually those with less power resent the lack of input they have and find ways to compete with the decision-maker. Kids get part-time jobs so they can have their own money. Homemakers get jobs outside the home so they can have more say in the family's finances.

But families still don't talk. They just argue.

No one knows how to avoid the stress. We want to manage our money well. We want to live within our means. We want to clear up our debts and have a little extra to fall back on.

We just don't know how.

And if we do know, we can't seem to apply our knowledge. Unexpected emergencies, newly discovered needs, new interests and activities have us constantly tearing our family budget into little pieces and holding our heads in despair.

► *Money Madness*

If all the ordinary stresses weren't enough, teenagers bring their own special stresses to the family's finances.

Kids know money is power. For them, it represents the doorway to self-determination. The idea of having "my own money to spend on anything I want" symbolizes much more than the actual buying potential they get from an allowance or part-time job.

We're constantly told teenagers have great purchasing power. The kids, themselves, tell us they never have enough money. It's all a matter of perspective. For kids, money is freedom—and you can never have enough freedom.

Three basic things tend to block kids from financial independence and add to the family's financial stress.

Ignorance—When the mother I saw in the mall said, "Your daughters don't know the first thing about money," she was more correct than she realized. Money is a symbol for kids—something they use to get something they want. That's about it.

The complexities of budgets, savings, interest, deficits, credits and so on often escape them. The difference between gross income and net income is a mystery. It's nearly impossible for a family of four to get by on $10,000 a year. But it sounds like a fortune to a teenager. And—try as you will—it's tough to get them to see it differently.

Sloppiness—You may think your child's room is a mess. But give him or her a checkbook for a couple of months, and the word "mess" will gain a whole new meaning.

Teenagers tend to be impulsive, emotional creatures. Their feelings greatly influence their decisions. And impulsive, emotional, feeling-oriented living is, by nature, messy. Naturally, these attitudes trickle down into kids' financial lives as well.

Wants vs. needs—"Mom, I need $15 for the ball game." "Dad, I have to have a new dress for the dance."

How often do we hear requests like these from our kids? And how often do they set off major family fights? As parents, we realize kids demand we satisfy their wants, not just their needs.

People really need food, shelter, companionship, love, forgiveness, education and a sense of belonging. Beyond that, most every request involves wants—not needs.

But you can't really blame kids. Listen to adults talk, and you hear much the same mumbo jumbo—my personal needs, my career needs, my financial needs, my sexual needs, my privacy needs, my creative needs, my spiritual needs, my aesthetic needs.

Is it any wonder our kids tell us they "have to have" this or "will die without" that? Can we really blame them for feeling so strongly about the things they want? Or for being so disappointed when they don't get those things?

► *Money Management*

The good news is all of this stress can be either overcome, avoided or at least dealt with in positive, healthy ways.

Learn when enough is enough. True, it's tough to be satisfied. It often seems like everyone around us has more than we do. We tend to convince ourselves that if we only had this or that we'd really be happy.

This argument is, of course, absolutely untrue. Once we get this or that, another this or that will be out there beckoning, "Buy me! Buy me!"

The happiness that comes from ownership is, at best, fleeting and, at worst, idolatrous. The psalmist realized this when he wrote in Psalm 23, "The Lord is my shepherd, I shall not want."

Owning things; buying things; getting new, better, improved things is fun. No one denies that. But in the end, buying doesn't lead to happiness. Things wear out, get stolen, get lost, go out of style or become dull.

As Christians, we know true happiness comes from our relationship with God and our neighbor. If we really believe our lives are shepherded by a loving, gentle God and not by our credit cards and bank accounts, we'll be free from want.

Then we'll be happy.

Believe you are what God has made you. Before you earned your first cent, brought home your first paycheck or owned your first teething ring, God declared you valuable and acceptable. And nothing has changed since then. You're still a valuable, acceptable, worthy person. How much you

Family Fund Fun

Use the following activities to help your family think about money and how your family spends it.

You're a winner! Each member of your family has just won $1,000. You have one week to use it as you wish. But at the end of the week your family will be required to donate $1,100 to charity. What will you do? Have each member of the family come up with a plan and work it out on paper for the week. Compare what happens after a week and see how your plans worked.

You've been deserted. You're a mother of two. You don't have a job and your husband has deserted you. How will you make it? As a family project, find out how much such a person could expect to get from government social services and local agencies. Then find the mother a job and child care, and plan her budget. Could you live on such a budget?

No job, no cash—Imagine your family suddenly has no income. You have two weeks before you can get government aid. What will you do? How will you eat? How will you pay your bills? Discuss strategies and priorities in your family.

Food-stamp family—Find out how much a family your size receives in food stamps. Try to eat on that amount for a week. What is it like? Challenge families of your youth group to do the same. And consider donating the difference between your regular grocery bill and the food stamp level to a local food bank.

earn or own has absolutely nothing to do with it.

When we accept that truth, we're freed from power struggles over who earns more money. We can get a job outside the home, be a homemaker or take a lower-paying job without having to determine who makes more and is therefore more valuable.

If we accept God's grace in our financial lives, we can share the problems, responsibilities, joy and celebrations equally—as a family.

Take time to talk. Talking, not fighting, is how we teach our kids financial responsibility. Plan your money talk. Set a date to sit down with the whole family and lay out the whole financial picture.

Planning a family budget together helps overcome financial stress in several ways:

- No one person has total responsibility for making financial decisions. Everyone has a voice—from the one who supplies the most money to the one who supplies the least. There's no need for power struggles.
- A budget makes finances concrete for children and teenagers who have trouble dealing with abstractions. With a budget, they can see where the money comes from and where it goes.
- It gives everyone in the family a firm basis for planning individual purchases. Everyone knows the money situation.
- It keeps you from being the "heavy" who always has to say no. You don't have to say, "No, we can't afford it." Rather, you can say, "We didn't plan it into the budget for this month."
- Unexpected windfalls and paid-off debts can become celebrations for the whole family.
- A budget teaches teenagers the importance of self-control in financial planning. This experience will be useful when it's time for them to create their personal budgets.
- It gives you a structure for putting financial management skills to work. With the structure in place, you aren't faced with hundreds of financial questions each day. The answers are in the budget.
- Finally, a budget helps you live within your means.

As someone once said, "The difference in financial happiness and financial distress is $1. Spend $1 less than you make, and you have happiness. Spend $1 more than you make and you have distress."

The "Monthly Family Budget" worksheet on page 64 can help your family get started on a budget. It's designed for a family of four, but is adaptable for almost any family. Before you begin, review these hints to make it work:

- Don't fill out the budget and hand it to family members. Make it a family project to come up with a budget.
- Don't argue. If there's a difference of opinion about how much money needs to be allocated for something, send everyone out to gather evidence to back up differing claims, such as canceled checks and receipts. Use the evidence to reach a consensus.
- Don't be too tight. Bare-bones budgets depress everyone. The goal here is to share information—not guilt.
- Be realistic. Don't count on things going better or money falling into your lap in the future.
- Keep it simple. Basically, teenagers understand money comes in and goes out. Where it comes from, and how and why it gets there may muddle things unnecessarily.

Teach your kids about finances. In her book *Children of Fast-Track Parents*, Andrée Aelion Brooks writes: "Money . . . is so much more available to kids these days that understanding how to handle it has to be a fundamental part of any upbringing. Yet it rarely is. A random sampling of 613 teenagers conducted in 1987 by Money magazine found a severe lack of sophistication about such basic matters as investments, taxes, and debt-service costs."[3]

Kids learn financial responsibility and self-control in three ways:

- From parents—While preachers and Sunday school teachers can talk about Christian stewardship, it's up to parents to show their kids how it works.

Check your spending habits closely. If you're an impulse buyer, recreational or therapeutic shopper, or sloppy bookkeeper, ask yourself what kinds of lessons you're teaching your kids.

Monthly Family Budget

Monthly Income

Income Sources

1. ______________________ $ __________

2. ______________________ $ __________

3. ______________________ $ __________

4. ______________________ $ __________

Total Monthly Income	$ __________

Monthly Expenses

Living Expenses

Mortgage payment or rent $ ________

Utilities $ ________

Phone $ ________

Gasoline $ ________

Car maintenance $ ________

Taxes $ ________

Insurance $ ________

Work expenses (parking, transportation, lunches) $ ________

Groceries $ ________

Medical expenses $ ________

Household expenses $ ________

Clothing $ ________

School supplies/fees $ ________

School lunches/snacks $ ________

Family entertainment $ ________

Grooming (haircuts, permanents) $ ________

Miscellaneous (pets, gifts, garden) $ ________

continued

Credit Payments (credit cards, loans)

1. ______________________________ $ __________
2. ______________________________ $ __________
3. ______________________________ $ __________
4. ______________________________ $ __________
5. ______________________________ $ __________
6. ______________________________ $ __________

Donations

Church $ __________ Charity $ __________

Savings

For emergencies $ ________

For long-term (college, retirement) $ ________

For short-term (Christmas, special purchases) $ ________

For fun (holidays, vacations) $ ________

Personal Allowances

Name: ______________________________ $ __________

Name: ______________________________ $ __________

Name: ______________________________ $ __________

Name: ______________________________ $ __________

Total Monthly Expenses $ __________

Total monthly expenses shouldn't exceed total monthly income. If it does, it's time to make some adjustments.

Do you save money regularly? What percentage of your income do you set aside for future goals? for charity and church-giving? Is it fair to expect your kids to do better than you do?

● From managing their own money—We teach our kids little and we cause ourselves undue stress when we constantly dole out bucks to them. Five dollars for this, $10 for that, $2 for the next thing. We become resentful and so do they. Everyone is served better if kids know how much money they'll have each month and can budget it themselves.

Allowance? Yes, I think an allowance is a good idea. How much depends on where you live, the cost of living in your area, your family's total income, and how much responsibility your teenager is ready to accept.

But instead of just giving kids money to spend randomly, help them learn to manage the money they have. Teach them the skills and self-discipline they'll need as they become responsible for more money.

Alida Rockefeller, a daughter of millionaire John Rockefeller III, tells how her family taught her money management. "There were three little jewelry boxes. I got fifteen cents to spend, fifteen cents to save, and fifteen cents to give away. Every Christmas my father would sit down with me and we'd decide who I'd give the [money] in the third box to . . . It was a real ritual, one of the times we were closest."[4]

Your total budget and your children's allowances may be quite different. But the Rockefellers' system is a good model.

● From their jobs—This is a controversial point, and one I approach with great caution. Part-time jobs during high school have both positive and negative consequences to consider:

+ A part-time job can help teach a teenager responsibility.

− But there's no guarantee that it will.

+ A part-time job can help a teenager save for college.

− But kids spend most of the money they earn on entertainment and clothing.

+ A part-time job can be a way to mature socially.

− But it can also throw kids into situations they aren't yet ready to handle. They'll be working with adults who are neither teachers nor parents.

+ A part-time job can conquer boredom and inactivity.

− But so can church and school functions that will be missed because of the job.

+ A part-time job can take some of the strain off family finances.

− But so can spending less. And a part-time job may require uniforms, medical expenses, travel expenses and extra expenditures.

+ A part-time job can help a teenager learn independence.

− But so can any parent who's willing to let his or her child make decisions and accept the consequences of those decisions.

Probably any lessons that can be learned from a part-time job can be just as easily learned from church, school and parents—without the added hassles and problems jobs often bring to families.

If your teenager wants to earn extra money, fine. That's probably a good sign. Help him or her become an entrepreneur—by starting a lawn-mowing or babysitting service; or becoming a free-lance gardener or dog walker or shrub trimmer or garage painter or car washer. Managing a business is real responsibility.

If your child insists on taking a "real" part-time job, set limits to help keep the job in its proper perspective. Consider these possible school-year parameters:

- not more than 15 hours per week on the job;
- not more than three hours in one weeknight;
- not more than two weeknights per week;
- not more than half a day on Saturday;
- no dropping previous commitments; and
- maintain a certain grade-point average.

And remember, a boss is not a parent, a teacher or a youth counselor. A boss's first order of business is business. Your teenager will need strong support from home when even a well-meaning boss urges him or her to bend your rules by staying late or working extra hours to help out.

Know and teach the difference between wants and needs. It's up to you. Your church will support your efforts. But it's your job. It can be done in six easy steps:

● Know the difference yourself. Decide early what your family really needs. Plan these things into your time, energy and budget.

From time to time talk about your wants, and encourage other family members to do the same. Be serious about them, but be silly too. List even the outrageous things you'd like to have. This will help keep everyone aware of the difference.

● Believe in the difference yourself. As parents, it's our responsibility to provide for our children's needs. It's not our responsibility to provide for all their wants.

As simple and self-evident as that may seem to many of us, it comes as tremendous, revolutionary, wonderful news to others. If you're one of these latter types, say it over and over again until you believe it. Then move to the next step.

● Stay calm under fire. "But Mom, everybody's wearing Shmuck jeans now. I'll look like a total idiot if I don't get some. They're only $45."

It's easy to lose your cool when your kids make what seem to be unreasonable demands on your financial resources. Do whatever it takes to remain calm. Count to 10. Take a deep breath. Say a brief prayer. Tell your teenager you'll have an answer in 15 minutes.

● Stick with the family budget. You might handle the designer jeans situation this way: "Connie, there's only $25 in our budget for blue jeans this month. And these designer jeans cost $45. I wish there was more money, but there just isn't."

● Offer options. Follow the previous statements with something like this: "We have a few options here. One, you can decide to be happy with regular jeans. Two, you can wait until next month, and we'll save this $25 until then so you can afford the $45 pair. Or three, you can add $20 of your own money to the $25 to make up the difference."

● Finally, bring your teenager into the decision-making process. Ask simply, "Which one do you want to do?" And then go along with whatever option he or she chooses—even if it wasn't one you would've chosen.

Sure, there may be complications. Your teenager may pout or storm around or accuse you, life and God of being unfair. She may say the family budget is tilted against her. He may be mad because life isn't going the way he would have it go if he were in charge.

That's okay. One rule in every household should be, "You aren't required to like the rules." Even we parents are sometimes frustrated by rules and budgets and other limits. But that's the way it goes.

If you feel yourself slipping, return to the first step and stay calm. Don't take it personally—these are growing pains. They, too, shall pass.

► *Money Manipulation*

Even with your careful teaching, you need to be prepared for the many ways your teenager may try to bend the budget. Your teenager will have several tactics.

"I'll take it out of my savings." This is a tough suggestion. What agreement was made about savings when the account was opened? Does the situation constitute an emergency? Were you given veto power over your child's money—and do you have a right to exercise that kind of power? Better to deal with these issues *before* they come up.

"Can you loan me the money?" Or "Can you give me an advance on next month's allowance?" These options are sometimes possible, but they should be done as strict business deals. How will the debt be paid? Will it be worked off? Doing what? Will it be taken out of next month's allowance? When? You don't need to sign papers, but be clear that a deal has been agreed to by everyone concerned. And writing down the exact amount will help avoid disagreements at payback time.

Of course, if there isn't money available to loan or advance, be honest about it. "We didn't budget any extra money to make loans or advances this month." See, it's not you being mean. It's the budget being fixed.

"Ple-e-e-e-e-e-ase!" This is the toughest response to

refuse. He puts his arm around you and, maybe, lays his head on your shoulder and gets that puppy-dog, little-boy look on his face.

And, *boing*, he's your little boy, turned into your pal. Or she's Dad's little princess, turned into Dad's pride.

Okay, be a softy. Give him or her the money—as a gift out of love.

And, for heaven's sake, tell your teenager why you're giving in! Tell him or her where the money's coming from. "I'll pack my lunch next week, and we can use the money I budgeted for my lunches."

This explanation is probably the most loving thing you can do. You're teaching your child that money comes *from* somewhere—in this case, from your sacrifice. No guilt, just a healthy dose of reality.

And reality is often the best cure for financial stress.

Endnotes

[1]Dolores Curran, *Stress and the Healthy Family* (San Francisco: Harper & Row, 1985), 62.

[2]Kate Greer, "Today's Parents: How Well Are They Doing?," Better Homes and Gardens, (October 1986), 36-46.

[3]Andrée Aelion Brooks, *Children of Fast-Track Parents* (New York: Viking Penguin, 1989), 114.

[4]Quoted in Brooks, *Children of Fast-Track Parents*, 119.

CHAPTER 5

And in This Corner: Conflict, Arguments and Fights

Jogging with Dick made me a good listener. He usually ran so fast that talking, for me, was out of the question. Breathing was about all I could manage.

Today was worse than usual.

We'd passed my three-mile limit, but Dick was just warming up to his run—and his subject. I stopped, bent over with my hands on my knees and tried to keep from passing out. Dick ran in place as he talked.

"Jason's driving me crazy," he said.

I grunted. It was the best I could do under the circumstances.

"He argues with me about everything. If I say the sky is blue, he says green. If I say black is black, he says it's white."

I managed to moan, "Jason's what, a sophomore?"

"A junior . . . The kid is off the wall!" he said, flailing his arms. "You ready yet?"

I nodded and started off at a slow jog, hoping he'd slow down a little. He did. But he kept talking.

"He seems to resent the slightest little things. Even the positive stuff. Last week I complimented him on how he looked, and you know what he did? He rolled his eyes! Rolled his eyes, for crying out loud. I asked when he was going to mow the grass, and he blew up!"

"He doesn't like to do chores," I said, trying to be helpful.

"What chores? I pay him to mow the yard! I provide the lawn mower, I pay for the gas, I beg him to do the mowing, remind him when it's time and pay him for doing it. I guess I'm supposed to be thankful for the opportunity."

The more he talked, the faster he ran. Finally, he put on a burst of speed and left me in the dust. The stress was just too much for jogging to take care of. He needed to run it off.

As I lay in the front yard of a neighbor's house—catching my breath—I tried to picture Dick's family.

Jason had two younger brothers. One a freshman, the other in junior high school. His mother was a homemaker and volunteered a lot at the church and school. From the outside, you'd think this was a normal, happy American family. From the outside, you couldn't see the stress.

In fact, Dick's family *is* a normal American family, experiencing what nearly every family experiences: conflicts, arguments and fights.

Jason's a teenager. He's involved in the natural and healthy business of stretching and thinning the parent-child bond. Eventually, it'll break and he'll emerge from adolescence as an independent adult.

Arguing, challenging and questioning are natural ways our kids establish their independence. And if we think for a few minutes, we wouldn't have it any other way. As a character in a movie once said, "If everyone got along with their parents, no one would ever move out. And nobody wants that."

But the process is stressful for Jason, his dad and probably the whole family. The fact that it's normal doesn't make it easy to live with. And it surely isn't the stuff nice, cozy relationships are built on.

Or is it?

In reality, how you handle conflicts with your teenager may determine what kind of relationship you have with him or her as an adult. Right now you're building that future relationship.

What Do You Fight About?

Just about anything that comes up is fertile ground for conflict between parents of teenagers. Check the areas in the list below that you fight about with your teenager. Add other areas not listed.

- ☐ Car use
- ☐ Chores
- ☐ Friends
- ☐ Eating habits
- ☐ Personal appearance
- ☐ Money
- ☐ College
- ☐ Personal habits
- ☐ Holidays
- ☐ ______________
- ☐ Curfews
- ☐ Clothes
- ☐ Dates
- ☐ Bathroom use
- ☐ Politics
- ☐ Homework
- ☐ Language
- ☐ Recreation
- ☐ Part-time job
- ☐ ______________
- ☐ Grades
- ☐ Telephone use
- ☐ Music
- ☐ Schedules
- ☐ Religion
- ☐ Exercise
- ☐ Values
- ☐ Vacation
- ☐ Sex
- ☐ ______________

When Campus Life magazine asked teenagers what they fight about with their parents, these answers came out on top:

1) Money;

2) Responsibilities at home;

3) Clothes (with mother); and

4)Telephone use (with father).

Take one of the top three areas you fight about. Evaluate whether your fights are generally positive or negative, using the principles in this chapter as guidelines. Pinpoint any problem areas, and work to overcome those barriers to healthy conflict.

I know people who like to euphemize everything they do. They don't sweat; they glisten. They don't eat; they dine. They don't fight; they have discussions.

Baloney.

If you're a parent, you fight. You want A, and your kid wants Z. Battle lines are drawn and shots are fired. And, well, it's a fight, pure and simple.

The question isn't whether or not to fight. The question is whether your fights build each other up or tear each other down. But before you can fight in constructive ways, you've got to overcome some barriers that make family fights destructive. Let's look at areas that can lead to destructive fighting and how to deal with them constructively.

► *Discipline*

When I was little, I lived next door to Stevie. Stevie was a mean kid. He bit me—on the arms, the hands, the fingers and, once, even on the head. No reason. No provocation. He just liked to bite.

I'd cry and show my mother the marks. And she'd confront Stevie's mother. Stevie's mom would put on a sad grin, shrug her shoulders and say, "Stevie's a bad boy. I don't know what to do with him."

Mom and I had several ideas, but she never asked us.

None of us want to be perceived as "Stevie's mother." We want other parents to stand in awe of how well-mannered, well-behaved and well-disciplined our children are. We want the world to know we're in control.

And therein lies the problem.

Discipline is not synonymous with control. They're often opposites. The word "control" means to check or stop by a countermove. While that may sometimes be necessary, it's hardly the last word in parenting teenagers.

The word "discipline" means to instruct or give knowledge. It comes from the same word as disciple. Jesus didn't try to stop his disciples' thinking with countermoves. He disciplined them. That is, he taught them and gave them knowledge.

When Carl, a 15-year-old in my church, let his grades

Are You a Fair Fighter?

Most of us aren't completely lucid when we're fighting. It's hard to evaluate our fighting technique in the middle of a fight. Use the following self-test to evaluate yourself after you've had a family fight. Circle the appropriate response to each question.

1. Did you feel the need to do something to control your teenager?	Yes	No
2. Did you shout more than twice?	Yes	No
3. Did you use broad generalizations such as "you always" or "you never"?	Yes	No
4. Did you bring up something that happened earlier you've been stewing about?	Yes	No
5. Did you feel a surge of anger about something that happened to you when you were a teenager?	Yes	No
6. Did you become violent in word or deed? throwing, hitting, threatening, kicking?	Yes	No
7. Did "winning" the argument seem important to you?	Yes	No
8. Did you say something you now regret?	Yes	No
9. Did you establish rules that, in retrospect, seem unreasonable?	Yes	No
10. Did you feel silly or ashamed after the fight?	Yes	No

If you answer yes to three or more of these questions, work on specific ways to make your fights more constructive. Use the suggestions in this chapter to get you started.

drop below his capabilities, his parents hit the ceiling. No television. No dates. No ball games. No extracurricular activities. No telephone. No fun until the grades improved.

The resulting emotional explosion could've leveled the entire city. Fights, accusations, recriminations, screaming matches and hurt feelings shot through the household. Finally, the family came to me—more to be a referee than a counselor and pastor.

After a lot of talking, Carl admitted he understood his parents' concern about his grades. Mom and Dad agreed they understood Carl's feelings about the severe controls they'd placed on him.

I asked, "Carl, how can your parents help you bring your grades back up?"

His answer was amazing: Put controls on his extracurricular activities, help him budget his time, remind him about schedules—all more reasonable versions of the restrictions his parents had imposed.

The difference? Before, Mom and Dad had been trying to control him. Now, they were teaching him how to discipline himself by giving him disciplines of his own.

Before they were controlling. Now they were disciplining.

Relationships are built on discipline, not control. In fact, trying to control another person is the quickest way to undermine a relationship and push that person to rebel.

Teenagers expect—and want—discipline. In survey after survey, they don't ask for lax or easy discipline. Quite the contrary, they ask for "firm but fair" discipline. Use these tips in disciplining your kids.

Be firm. Agree to rules in advance, and stand by them. Make sure your teenager knows the rules and understands how to interpret them. And make sure you know the rules and all possible interpretations. Also, be clear about the consequence that will be imposed if a rule is broken. Then hold fast.

Be fair. Keep your word. Don't take away something you've given or promised. Do only what you said you'd do—no more, no less.

If the consequence for poor grades is no television until

the grades come back up, then unplug the television. But don't take away the car too. That may be firm, but it isn't fair. It wasn't part of the original agreement.

Teach with discipline. Remember that to discipline means to teach. Make sure your teenager understands what's at stake and why a particular action is being imposed. Why is it important? What's to be learned? Is it being learned?

When your teenager comes home 15 minutes after the agreed upon deadline, listen to her story before you impose the penalty. It may have been due to something beyond her control. If it was, point out how she could have avoided such a situation in the first place.

But lighten up on the penalty. Showing her how and why to take responsibility for her own life is important. But don't handle it in the same way you'd handle willful defiance of a curfew.

Learn to compromise. Every healthy relationship involves give-and-take. We give up something we want for the sake of our relationship with the other person. The same holds true in our relationships with our kids.

You say $10 is enough allowance. He wants $20. You compromise: $10 free and clear with opportunities to earn the other $10.

You say midnight. She says 2 a.m. You compromise: 1 a.m. with a call around 11.

By compromising we demonstrate to our kids the give-and-take necessary to make a relationship work.

Wait and watch. Sometimes the hardest part of parenting is to do nothing—to step back and let our kids be wrong. We give our best advice, we warn them, talk to them, plead with them. And then all we can do is wait and watch. We give up control and let them bear the responsibility for their actions.

When I decided to sell my used car while in college and start making payments on a new subcompact, my parents didn't like the idea at all. But they didn't forbid it.

My dad was gracious enough not to say, "I told you so," when I had to sell it and get another used one. Letting me make a mistake of this magnitude was a valuable form of discipline.

Worship together. Some churches forget that families need to do things together. Adults go to worship while kids go to Sunday school. And everyone meets to argue about lunch afterward.

I think this approach is a terrible mistake. Families should worship together. When we sit together in worship, we're reminded that we're all under a higher authority than ourselves. When we praise God together in song and prayer, and when we hear the Word proclaimed, we're reminded of who's really in charge. Our relationships to each other and the world are put in proper perspective.

Family devotions, prayer and Bible study can also help us head off fights before they happen. These family times remind us life isn't a battle between parent and child. Rather, for Christians, it's a united effort to serve God and our neighbor. Devotions can unite us as the whole family receives "discipline" from God.

► *Unfinished Business*

Unfinished business remains between you and your teenager when past fights are never fully resolved. So you bring up the issues later, during a new fight.

"No! You can't go to that party. Last time you went to a party you stayed out late and I was worried sick. I didn't get to bed till 2 a.m. and I slept through the alarm and was two hours late to work! I can never trust you to do what you say." Lots of unfinished business.

Bring up unfinished business, and your fights go haywire. They go off in all directions, bounce off things, make hairpin turns—completely out of control.

The best way to deal with unfinished business is to not have any. When an issue becomes a fight, finish it and be done with it. When the fight's over, ask yourself and your teenager, "Are we done with this?" If not, keep working until you are.

Agree in advance that whenever you fight you won't bring up old business. Use a code word that signals when someone has broken the agreement. A friend of mine says she and her husband use the word "Boink!" They'll be fighting along and someone will say, "Oh, yeah! Well, last week when we were . . ." and the other one will say, "Boink!"

Often, that interjection alone will end the fight, which dissolves in a hail of laughter.

▶ Accusations

When we fight, we tend to talk about each other. "You did this! . . ." "Well, you did that! . . ." "But you did something else! . . ." "Oh, but you . . ."

I once heard a counselor say, "When you talk about me, you tell me more about you than you do about me." He was right. When we fight, it's because of feelings we have, but we usually don't talk about those feelings. We talk about the person we're fighting with. Naturally, that person feels defensive and, in turn, talks about us. So we feel defensive and . . .

Get the picture?

Talk about yourself. Use "I" statements. Say:

- When you ______________, I feel ______________.
- I want ______________________________________.
- I'm willing to__________________________________.

Encourage the other person to respond with "I" statements as well.

Marriage counselors have used formulas like that for years. Use it and encourage your kids to use it. It turns a fight into work toward a common goal. Both people express how they feel, how they want to feel and what they're willing to do to get what they want.

All that's left is to work out the details.

▶ Anger

Every time I try to recruit someone for a job in the church, I run into unique people. You probably know some of them. They're the ones who can't say no without first getting mad.

"Hi, this is Dean, and I was wondering if you'd be able to be on the Something-or-Other Committee this year," I say,

"Oh, I wish I could help, honey. But I'm so busy. And I've already done so much. First was the party . . . Then the trip . . . Then . . . I can't believe you asked. I really can't help with your homework."

putting a smile into my voice.

"Well, Dean," they begin, "I'll tell you something. I just finished being chairman of the Whatever-It-Was Committee, and I don't think I want to do that again for a long time. Those people drove me crazy with their bickering and fighting. I would've thought church people would behave themselves better, but I was sadly disappointed. Can you believe . . ."

They're on a roll now. Look out!

". . . people who call themselves Christians could act like that? I mean, I'm a busy person, and I have important things to do. And they have the gall to put me through that! Who do they think they are, anyway? How dare they? And how dare you even ask me to do such a thing? Who do you think you are? . . . and . . . and . . ."

You get the picture. A simple no would've done nicely.

The same principle holds true for parents. We don't have to be mad to say no. We don't have to be mad to demand our rights as people or as parents. In fact, we don't *have* to be mad at all—ever.

We choose to be.

We feel ourselves getting angry. We feel the anger coming, invite it in, grab it, swallow it and *boom*!—we're angry! Next thing we know, the anger takes over, and we say things that don't make sense, things we can't take back and things we probably wish we wouldn't have said in the first place.

The key to dealing with anger is not to get angry. Anger is a feeling that should inform our behavior, not control it. If you feel yourself getting angry try these actions.

Talk about your anger. "I'm feeling angry right now because . . ." Then let your teenager respond to your feeling. Talking about anger is always more constructive than demonstrating it.

Walk away. Don't make an important decision when you're angry. Say: "I'm too angry to decide about this right now. I'll decide what to do after I've cooled down."

Take a walk. Lift weights. Work at cooling off. Don't use the time to seethe and boil. Use it to think.

Dick—from our opening story—jogged when the stress got to be too much. By the time he returned home, his anger had cooled and he could deal calmly with his son.

Change the geography. If your teenager's room makes you angry because it's so messy, that's not a good place to talk about grades. You'll end up letting the anger about the room slip into your discussion about grades. Go to the living room for this discussion. Save the "room discussion" for another time.

A friend irons shirts when she's mad at the kids. She talks to them while she irons. She says the ironing board serves as a barrier between her and the kids, and ironing helps relieve some of the stress. She takes it out on the shirts, not the kids.

Do all those old things that seem like clichés. Count to 10. Take three deep breaths. Lie down for a few minutes. Play the piano. Do whatever it takes to work out your anger before you deal with the matter at hand.

Suppressed anger is almost as stressful as demonstrated anger. Give yourself a safe, creative outlet for your feelings.

It's said that my great-grandmother never raised her voice in anger. But you knew when she was mad because of all the fresh baked bread in the kitchen. She needed to knead, I suppose.

If you do get angry, apologize. Otherwise, both the anger and what you said in anger will remain a barrier between you and your child. Once you've apologized—and meant it—you can deal with the issue that brought on the anger.

► *Wounded Memories*

When I was in the eighth grade, I was so uncoordinated I couldn't do jumping jacks. I had trouble just running up and down the gym floor. And I certainly couldn't dribble a basketball.

That last shortcoming amused my physical education teacher. He thought it'd be neat for the whole class to watch me try.

So he stopped the class, gave me a basketball and told me to dribble down the gym floor and back while everyone watched—and laughed.

Helping Teenagers Deal With Anger

I know how to handle my anger. But my kids don't. They don't fight fair or constructively! What can I do? Good question. Here are some tips:

1. When fighting, don't let your teenager bring other things into the fight. Say: "We're not talking about that. We're talking about this. We'll talk about that later if you want."

2. Give kids space to be angry. "You seem to be getting angry. I feel that way myself. Let's take a break and come back to this after supper."

3. Don't get defensive. Statements such as "You don't care about my problems" or "You don't understand" are intended to make you prove otherwise. Ignore them, and stick with the subject at hand.

4. Make sure your kids are getting adequate exercise. Sometimes anger is just an easy outlet for excess energy.

5. Explore the anger. Ask: "Why are you feeling angry? What exactly are you angry about?" You may be surprised at what you discover! The anger may not be about the car but about your teenager feeling untrusted.

6. Break the anger down. Anger is complex. It may come from exasperation, indignation, exhaustion, humiliation or any number of things. They're all fairly solvable—once you identify them.

7. Honor the anger. Remember that anger is an honest, healthy human emotion. Without it, many wrongs would never be righted. What's necessary is a healthy outlet for anger.

Needless to say, I was humiliated. I was teased about that incident until the day we moved from the school district three years later. And I still get a sort of upset stomach if I think about it very long. Even writing about it is painful for me.

I never trusted coaches after that. Oh, I played sports. I even lettered in football, basketball and track in high school. But I never really trusted my coaches. I knew what kind of cruelty they were capable of.

And I still do.

So I'm not anxious for my kids to play sports. I don't want them to be humiliated in front of their peers the way I was. In my rational moments, I know this fear is ridiculous. That was almost 30 years ago. Things have changed. Coaching and teaching methods have improved. And in my rational moments, I'm fine.

But when I'm fighting—when I'm less than rational—that's when the wounded memory of my eighth-grade coach comes drifting to the surface and causes problems.

Once, our family planned a weekend trip to see the autumn colors in southern Indiana. I managed to get Sunday off. The reservations were made and the money saved. Then my son, Ben, came home and announced his soccer coach had planned an unscheduled scrimmage again on Saturday. And he *really* wanted to play. I could see my mini-vacation vanishing.

Ben says he saw me put on my "fighting face," so he caught me before I could reach the telephone. He just wanted to remind me his coach was really a nice, sensitive, kind guy, and it wasn't necessary to yell at him.

He was right, of course. Coaches just get to me—I can't help it. So I calmly called and apologized that Ben wouldn't be at the scrimmage. The coach understood perfectly. We shouldn't give it another thought, he said. Have a good time.

If I'm not careful, I find myself fighting with that eighth-grade coach instead of my kids. Which, of course, won't help anyone—my kids, the coach or me.

Be aware of your own wounded memories and share them with your kids. This openness may not help you avoid those memories in a fight, but it lets your kids know why you act the way you do.

I've shared my eighth-grade coach story with my kids, and they think it's the most awful thing they've ever heard. And they understand that their dad is sometimes irrational when it comes to coaches. So they stay off the subject, or they help me with it when it comes up.

They're gentle with me.

► *Rebellion*

We've seen that questioning, challenging and arguing are normal, healthy things for teenagers to do. They're not fun, and they cause stress for the whole family. But with thought, care and prayer, we can help these normal adolescent behaviors become positive avenues for growth and maturation.

Rebellion, however, is a different story.

Rebellion—a pattern of willful, defiant rejection of parental love, concern and authority—is neither healthy nor normal. It's a symptom of a much deeper problem to be handled with the help of a trained, certified counselor.

Learn to identify these 10 early warning signs of rebellion in teenagers:

- a fascination with heavy metal music and images;
- a pattern of rule-breaking;
- a lack of empathy for siblings or pets;
- a fascination with satanism or the occult;
- identification with rebellious groups such as Skinheads, the Ku Klux Klan, Nazis or motorcycle gangs;
- a lack of concern for personal hygiene or appearance;
- a refusal to communicate with adults on even the most basic level;
- the presence of drugs, alcohol or drug paraphernalia;
- a lack of personal ambition; and
- long, unexplained absences from home or school.

Seeing one or two of these behaviors in isolated incidents might simply reflect your child's desire to experiment with different actions. But don't assume that. Get your teenager to talk about it. Discuss it casually and calmly if you can. Share your feelings.

If your discomfort persists—or if your child's behavior is blocking your family from functioning in a healthy way—get help.

Often, feelings of inadequacy and embarrassment cause us to delay asking for help. Don't let those feelings stop you. Your child's well-being and your own mental health may be at stake. Go to your pastor or your school principal immediately. If they can't help you, they'll direct you to someone who can.

► Relax

None of us likes to fight and argue—especially with someone we helped bring into the world. But we *will* argue, because we're each unique, and we each have unique needs.

The question isn't will we fight? The question is ***how*** will we fight?

By changing the question, family fights become less ominous. We don't have to worry whether fighting will tear us apart. Instead, we just work on learning to fight in ways that draw us together.

So relax. Learn how to fight right. And enjoy seeing your family grow closer as you work through your differences.

CHAPTER 6

Altered States: The Changing Parent-Child Relationship

As parents, we all want our children to become independent and self-sufficient adults. Yet we often find ourselves fighting the essential changes that are for growth and independence.

Why? Because the changes are painful and full of stress.

For about a dozen years, we've watched, waited, hoped, dreamed, diapered, washed, fed, taught, bandaged, doctored, laughed with and cried over these little, helpless, dependent people. Their lives have become our lives. Given the chance, we would've suffered their illnesses, endured their suffering, fought their fights and even taken a bullet for them.

And they returned our love. They cried when we left them. They called out for us when they were sick or injured. They hugged us when we returned from a trip. And they bragged to their friends about us. They wanted to be like us when they grew up.

But now—just a few years later—things have changed.

They reject our advice. They question our values. They spurn our help. We're an embarrassment to them. They don't want us around anymore.

This change causes tremendous emotional stress for

parents. Early childhood is stressful for parents, but at least we're in control. Adolescence seems to place us on the outside looking in.

It's not hard to imagine that when the prophet Hosea wanted to describe the broken relationship between God and Israel, he turned to his own experiences as the father of adolescent sons: "When Israel was a child, I loved him and out of Egypt I called my son. The more I called them, the more they went from me; they kept sacrificing to the Baals, and burning incense to idols. Yet it was I who taught Ephraim to walk, I took them up in my arms; but they did not know that I healed them" (Hosea 11:1-3).

Suddenly all relationships are turned upside down. Nobody warned us. Nobody told us the rules would change halfway through the game. The stress seems unendurable.

Parents are out; friends are in. Old friends are out; old enemies are in. Members of the opposite sex are no longer warned away, but actively sought after. Siblings who were worst enemies are now fast friends . . . for today.

And tomorrow, everything may be different.

In the wake of all these relational changes often lie the stresses of hurt feelings and rejected values. What should parents do? What should we say? How are we supposed to cope with all this? Should we try? It's so painful for everyone—parent and teenager. Is it worth it?

Maybe if we just keep our heads and duck low enough it'll blow over. Maybe it's just a phase they'll grow out of. Maybe this stress will pass and, someday, everything will get back to normal.

Maybe.

But phase or not, it's a very real, very authentic and very necessary time in our teenagers' lives. And they'll handle the stress of these times better and come through it healthier if we're there with them.

We can make the pain of these changes more bearable. Like the pain that runners feel when they lengthen their stride in a marathon, the pain of change can be understood as the pain of progress, achievement and strength.

The following seven principles can help us shift to that perspective.

► Principle #1: All Relationships Change

My wife is not married to the same person she was married to 20 years ago. Oh, sure, the name on the marriage license is the same. But I'm not.

I'm older and fatter and slower and probably a little more patient and a little less judgmental than I was back then. And a little less exciting.

Our relationship has changed too. We know what to expect from each other. We're at ease in each other's company. We let our hair down, lower our guard, say what's on our minds. Sometimes it may be dull. But mostly, it's nice. We'd look kind of silly if we constantly pawed each other like a couple of teenagers.

If my relationship with my wife has changed, why should I expect less of my relationship with my kids? As they grow and change, and as I grow and change, so will our relationship. It's inevitable. Trying to fight it, deny it or stop it is like trying to harness a whirlwind. It's impossible to do, and you just get hurt trying.

So be flexible. Learn to enjoy the changes in your kids.

Instead of becoming angry when your son seems to spend half his life in the shower, think of those days when you had to chase him down and drag him to the bathtub.

Instead of feeling rejected when your daughter insists on making her own mistakes, remember the times at the park when you thought she'd never learn to swing herself without a push from you.

You can help yourself come to terms with your child's independence by letting the independence benefit the family. Let your teenager participate more and more as an adult in the family's problems and celebrations. Encourage him or her to contribute.

As teenagers strive to become independent, make opportunities for them to try out their independence. Can Dola drive? Let her take over some of the taxi services. Can Keith cook? Ask him to cook a meal from time to time, and you take an evening off. Is Angela interested in clothing? Good. Let her take care of her own clothes for a change.

"Why don't you like your room anymore?
We fixed it up just for you."

Here's a helpful rule for tapping youthful independence to the family's advantage: The person in charge of laundry does laundry once per week. If you want to wear something that's now dirty, you must see to it that it gets to the laundry area. If it doesn't and you still want to wear it, you have to wash, dry and press it. Apply the same principle to other chores as well.

► *Principle #2: The Distancing Isn't Personal*

Your children aren't distancing themselves from you because they want to as much as because they have to. Nature has given them no choice.

Often, they'd love nothing more than to spend time with you. But their friends are important. Right now they're learning how to make and keep friends beyond their families. Without that skill, their adult lives will be sad and lonely indeed.

Kids may feel torn between their parents and their friends. Yelling at them, making them feel guilty about attending to their peer relationships and laying down ultimatums won't build up your relationship.

Instead of fighting the change, encourage it. Let your teenager know it's possible to have both friends and parents.

Invite your teenager's friends into your home. And make friends feel welcome by making sure there's food and drink available. Cookies and Cokes go a long way in making friends.

Watching a football game with your teenager and his or her friends lets you be together with a common interest in a non-threatening atmosphere. If football isn't your thing, try tennis. Or golf. Or a movie. Or *The Three Stooges*.

Even better, instead of trying to set up a big TV event, just have a seat while they're watching the tube. Bring some popcorn to share. Don't try to make conversation, just be with them. You'll be a hit.

► Principle #3: You Can't Always Trust Your Feelings

At my first church as a youth minister, I had an enormous junior high youth group—about a hundred kids. It was a wild and woolly bunch, full of spunk, spit and vinegar. Two of the eighth-grade boys were deaf and mute. They read lips and signed. I didn't, but we managed to communicate.

That spring I announced we'd be having a retreat. The theme would be human sexuality.

Kids came out of the woodwork. The 70 spaces on the bus were filling rapidly. And I noticed that the two deaf guys weren't signed up. So I gave the mother of one of them a call.

"Oh, yes, Peter told me about the retreat," she said, "but he won't be going. He just doesn't feel he's ready to deal with all that yet."

I thanked her and hung up the phone, pretty much accepting what she had said. But then I began to wonder. Isn't ready yet? Isn't ready for what? Wait a minute! I'd never met an eighth-grade boy who wasn't ready to talk about sex. Just because Peter's ears didn't work didn't mean the rest of him was non-functional.

So when I happened to see him at McDonald's one day, I asked, "Hey big guy, can't make it to the retreat, huh?"

He looked at the ground and shook his head. I patted him on the shoulder and told him I understood. Maybe next spring he'd feel more like going. He nodded somberly.

We separated, and just as I was finishing my Big Mac and fries, a napkin floated onto the table in front of me. Written on it was, "My mom won't let me go."

I looked up into Peter's sad eyes.

"Do *you* feel like you're ready?" I asked.

He nodded his head enthusiastically.

"What if I talk to her?" I offered.

He shook his head and bent to write on the napkin. "Do no good. She always does this. She's afraid for me."

Finally he sat down, and we continued to talk—me talking at his eyes; him writing on napkins. The story was an old one for Peter. The coach had said there was no reason he couldn't play football. They'd work something out so he could see or feel the signals being called.

Mom said no. He might get hurt.

Peter wanted to go to the junior high dance.

Mom said no. He'd only feel left out, because he couldn't hear the music.

Peter wanted to be in the school play.

Mom said no. He'd look silly signing his lines.

Practically the only thing his mother had let him do besides go to school was attend youth group.

When I looked at Peter I saw a big, handsome, athletically built, smart kid—who happened to be deaf. But when his mother looked at him, she saw her little boy—cheated out of his hearing, teased by mean little kids, hurt by insensitive adults. She'd do everything in her power to protect her little boy.

But in the process she was smothering him and denying him the opportunity to grow, because she couldn't see him as a growing teenager with needs, desires, urges and instincts like every other teenage guy in the world.

Peter didn't need someone to bandage his knees anymore. He needed someone to teach him about puberty and the way it was affecting his body. The caring he needed looked different, but it was still caring.

When your child becomes a teenager, it's natural to miss your little princess or your little prince. You'll feel grief about your old relationship. That's okay. It was a fun time and, chances are, you won't have it again. So go ahead and feel sad . . . for a while.

Then move on. Your kids need you here and now.

Like childhood, adolescence can be an exciting, invigorating, wonderful experience. You may not be Mommy and Daddy, but you're still Mom and Dad. You can still teach and feed and bandage and care for your children. Your concern just looks a little different now.

► *Principle #4: Worrying Is Normal . . . Up to a Point*

Worrying is what parents do. It's our prerogative. It's normal.

The trouble comes when worry and anxiety paralyze us and pollute our relationships. The trick is to let our kids know we worry about them without making our worry a burden they carry around.

Your teenager probably will tell you not to worry. You're just being silly, overprotective, smothering, and so on. That's okay. He or she still likes to know you care, so express your concerns.

And don't be defensive. You don't have to defend yourself for saying, "Be careful." You don't have to feel guilty about saying, "Call if you're going to be late." These things show you care.

On the other hand, you can't keep your kids in protective custody. You've had them for many years. It's time to see if what you've taught them did any good.

How can you tell when you've crossed over the line? when you're worrying too much? Ask yourself some questions when you're concerned about something your teenager wants to do:

● Is my concern reasonable? What are the odds of what I'm worrying about happening?

● Is what my child wants to do normal? Is it part of the maturing process? Is it something most kids want and should do at this age?

● If I say no to my child, will I deprive him or her of an opportunity for growth? When will another opportunity like this come along?

● Do I trust my teenager? How does he or she handle other, smaller things?

The answers to these questions may help you gauge whether your worries are reasonable.

Even if they are reasonable, however, you may have to give your teenager the freedom to do some things you worry about. The better you know your kids, the more you'll trust them and the less you'll worry.

► *Principle #5: Kids Have to Make Their Own Mistakes*

Think of the family as a circus. If your home is anything like mine, it won't be difficult. As parents, we want to be the ringmaster—to crack the whip, blow the whistle, shout orders. We want to be in charge—in control.

After all, we're older and more experienced. We've made mistakes, and we can save our kids a lot of pain if they'll only listen to us.

But that approach just doesn't work.

For a better model, we have to look above the three rings to the trapeze. Each trapeze act has a catcher and a flyer. The catcher's job is to be at the right place at the right time with arms strong enough to catch the flyer when he or she completes the double somersault with a full twist. The flyer's job, of course, is to fly and be caught.

Parents are the catchers.

Teenagers are the flyers.

The catcher says, "Be careful." But she doesn't say, "Don't fly." Neither does he say, "Fly, but don't fly too high and don't do the triple somersault with the double twist."

What the catcher says is, "Do your best and I'll be there to catch you. Just reach out your arms, and I'll be there."

We can't keep our kids from making mistakes. We can try, but if we insist, we'll drive a wedge between them and us. All we can do is be there for them . . . to catch them.

► *Principle #6: God Provides a Net*

You thought I forgot about the net, didn't you?

Sometimes even the catcher can't help. Sometimes the flyer's mistake is beyond the catcher's grasp. That's why there's a net.

God doesn't leave our children to fly without a net. It's not all left in the hands of the catcher/parent.

Teachers, ministers, friends, youth leaders, doctors, police, nurses, psychologists, neighbors—all of these people help form the net that can help catch our kids if they fall away from our grasp.

Am I Holding on Too Tightly?

Complete the following sentences in a way that most closely fits your own response.

1. When my child is 16, I'll . . .

a. be relieved to have another driver in the family.

b. worry when he or she goes out on the road alone or with friends.

c. not let him or her drive. Sixteen is too young—no matter what the law says.

2. I _________ find myself thinking about my teenager's early childhood years.

a. rarely

b. occasionally

c. often

3. When my teenager wants to make a decision I don't agree with, I . . .

a. don't worry about it. I trust my kids.

b. feel concerned about the problems my teenager may be bringing on himself or herself.

c. feel hurt and rejected.

4. My teenager's friends . . .

a. are a fun bunch.

b. are okay. But sometimes they can be a pain in the neck.

c. intrude on our family life and distract my teenager from what's really important.

5. As my teenager approached adolescence, I . . .

a. looked forward to it.

b. felt some anxiety.

c. was terrified and didn't know what to expect.

6. When my teenager wants to go out with friends, I . . .

a. feel glad he or she has good friends.

b. want to know who the friends are, where they're going, how they're getting there and when to expect them back.

c. try to prevent it whenever I can.

continued

7. When my kids make mistakes, I . . .
- a. feel bad for them, but know that's part of growing up.
- b. give them a hug and tell them I'm sorry things didn't work out.
- c. try to fix things up so they don't have to suffer too much.

8. I talk to my teenager's teachers . . .
- a. if they call me and ask to talk to me.
- b. at parent-teacher conferences and other occasions when it's appropriate.
- c. at least once every two or three weeks.

9. When I think of my teenager moving away from home, I . . .
- a. look forward to the peace and quiet.
- b. try to make the most of the time we have together.
- c. feel like crying.

10. If my teenager were to get in trouble at school, I . . .
- a. wouldn't worry too much. Everyone gets in trouble occasionally.
- b. would want to know the whole story and would talk to my child about it with an open mind.
- c. would be there in a flash to make sure my kid got a fair shake.

Tally your score using the following formula:
- 10 points for each a: ____________
- five points for each b: ____________
- One point for each c: ____________

Total score: ____________

Now evaluate your score:

80 to 100 points—You aren't holding on too tightly to your kids. You're giving them lots of space to grow. Be careful, though. Your laid-back style may come across as uncaring. Make sure you tell them you care about them and trust them. That's why you aren't always interfering with what they do.

40 to 79 points—You're about average. You worry about your kids, but you don't have them chained in the basement for their own protection. Try to maintain this balance. Concern, trust, support and help will see you and your kids through the hard times.

Less than 40 points—Loosen up a little. You're the classic example of the hovering parent. So your kids make some mistakes. In the long run, it'll be better for them if they suffer some knocks and learn from them.

Nurture relationships with these people. Bring them onto your parenting team. Without them, your kids are flying without a net.

Join the parent organization at school. Become an officer in the neighborhood watch program. Invite your neighbors to a cookout in your back yard. Invite the church youth group to your house for a party. Volunteer to help out at the school. Whatever it takes, get involved with the adults who are influencing your kids. Then when the need arises, you can talk to them.

You're all in this together.

► Principle #7: If We Would Have Our Kids, We Must First Give Them Up

What we cling to, we lose. What we let go of, we gain. I can't even count the number of times the Bible makes this point about life. Jesus said it about our own lives: "For whoever would save his life will lose it, and whoever loses his life for my sake will find it" (Matthew 16:25).

Remember the story of Abraham and Isaac?

Abraham was 100 years old when Isaac was born. He'd waited a very, very long time, and we can expect he doted over his son a great deal. Little Isaac was the apple of his eye. Then one day, God told Abraham to give up his son. Let go of him completely. Sacrifice him.

Now you and I don't worry too much about this story, because we know how it ends. But I remember the first time I heard it. It terrified me. How could God demand such a thing? How could Abraham say yes? I thought he loved his child!

And if Abraham—this nearly perfect man—could do such a thing, what might be expected of other parents? I was thankful my parents were probably not quite as perfectly obedient to God as Abraham.

Now—as an adult and a parent—I see the story in Genesis 22 differently. It tells us God blessed Abraham and Isaac after Abraham showed he was willing to part with his son.

There's something there for us as parents to think about.

How can God bless our children if we're unwilling to trust them to him? If we keep them for ourselves—protected, sheltered, safe from all life's harms—we deny the possibility that God may have a calling and a purpose for them beyond and greater than our own.

The lives of our children can be truly blessed only when we let them be. And when their lives are blessed by God, our relationship with them will be blessed.

CHAPTER 7

Something Completely Different: The Stress of Change

Sixth grade was the worst year of my life.

To start things off, we moved. Twice.

We were supposed to move to our new house in August, but it wasn't finished. So we moved into a rented house for three months. Then two months into the school year, we moved again.

With the moves came changes in neighbors, living conditions, schools, friends, rituals and routines.

In the fifth grade, we'd stayed in the same room all day and the teachers came to us. But in this new school—with all new peers—I had to move from room to room for every class. In the fifth grade I paid for my lunches in one lump sum at the beginning of the week. Now I had to keep track of my lunch money every day.

My brother Scot had gone to the same school and ridden the same school bus with me for the past three years. Now I had to go to school alone and ride a bus with a bunch of kids I didn't know.

As if all of this weren't enough, my body decided it was time to begin puberty. Suddenly, I no longer "hated" girls. Quite the contrary, I found them strangely attractive and fascinating. But the thought of talking to them terrified me. My body went haywire. My voice began doing weird things. I had strange, wonderful, troublesome thoughts concerning the cheerleaders and majorettes—all of whom treated me as if I were pond scum.

Then not long after we moved, Kirk, my best friend in my old school, was struck by a car and killed. I grew depressed, withdrew, stopped doing my homework, slept a lot, thought, tried to read, watched television, snapped at my family and spent most of my energy just trying to keep myself sane.

By the end of the year my personal stress had taken a heavy toll on the whole family. My parents considered sending me to a therapist or a private boarding school—anything to pull me out of my depression and get my life back on track.

Probably the thing that saved me was the church. Of all the things affecting my life at that time, the church was the only constant. Somehow we managed to stay in the same church. My friends there stayed the same. The minister was the same. The building, the Sunday school teachers, the old ladies with the strong perfume, the potluck dinners, the fussy choir director and the severe head usher—all the same.

They'll never know how important they were to me.

Amazingly, my experience isn't unique. Teenagers experience change at a mind-boggling rate. Three or four times a year they undergo changes that would exhaust any adult who had to handle as much in a year.

Usually kids have raw energy to handle all the change. They even need change to keep from getting bored. But they also need constants in their lives. A ship fulfills its purpose only when it sails. But it still needs an anchor and a home port.

Likewise, kids need the security of a strong anchor and a safe harbor. Without these, they're tossed about in a storm of stress that may threaten to drown them in emotional turmoil. And because they're part of our families, we feel the turbulence with them.

As parents, we can provide the safe harbor—the strong anchor—for our kids and families in these times of change. These come from a strong faith, solid preparation for unavoidable changes and companionship through changes that catch teenagers by surprise.

In this chapter, we'll look at some of the changes teenagers and families face, and ways to cope creatively with the changes.

► *Normal Changes*

Kids need change in their lives. Without change, kids become bored and lose interest. So they move from class to class, grade to grade, activity to activity, even sweetheart to sweetheart with relative ease—taking the changes in stride.

That kids need regular change, however, doesn't mean they're always equipped to handle it well. The very changes they seek can stress them and their families. You can help your teenager handle the stresses of normal changes in three major ways.

Help them anticipate change. To do this, offer gentle reminders that change has occurred in the past and will probably continue in the future.

The key word here is "gentle." This boyfriend may seem to be "the one." Perfect in every way. Everything your daughter could want in a future mate. But you've seen "perfect" boyfriends come and go. You won't help by making statements such as: "Oh, yeah, sure. This one will be just like all the others. You'll have a new one next week."

A more gentle reminder comes in the shape of genuine interest. "You seem really happy with Jeff. What do you think makes him special? How is he different from other guys you've dated?"

Puberty means changes in your teenager's body, feelings and outlook. You can help your child anticipate these changes.

Make sure your kids get a thorough education about human sexuality. Teaching them yourself is, of course, the best way. But if you find you just can't, help your church organize a class in human sexuality. Knowing about puberty is half the secret of handling it.

Helping our kids anticipate change doesn't remove the stress, but it can help ease it.

Talk about change. At the dinner or breakfast table, or while you're driving, mention changes you've noticed in your teenager. Give him or her a chance to reflect on how changes affect his or her life.

Sometimes a simple statement from you is all it takes. "Last year you didn't seem to like soccer. But I've noticed you really seem to enjoy it this year."

Or ask a general question for the whole family to discuss. "How is your life different now from the way it was a year ago? How do you feel about the changes?" Or "How do you think your life will be different a year from now?"

When we reflect on changes we've undergone, we realize they didn't kill us. We discover we're strong enough to handle change and sometimes, prosper in the midst of it.

Be an empathetic listener. The stress of change can make tempers flare. Kids may resent the changes life forces on them. Yet there's often nothing they or we can do about the changes except endure.

But it's easier to endure unwanted and painful changes if we have someone to dump on from time to time. Give your kids space to be angry in. When they snap at you, take a deep breath before you snap back. Try to identify the pain behind that anger.

When I was little we used to visit my grandparents' farm. My brother, sister and I would spend hours crawling up the chicken runs into an old hen house that had been converted to a tool shed.

Then one summer I crawled up the run and found I could no longer fit through the little hole that led into the shed. All I could do was stand and watch my siblings laugh and play.

Naturally, I took my anger out on them. They were "stupid babies playing baby games." But I was really angry with myself for being so darned big.

When my grandmother noticed my outburst, she didn't try to correct my behavior. Instead, she took me aside and showed me how to make a slingshot—an activity more suited to older, bigger kids. It was nice to have an adult who understood my feelings and didn't feel the need to lecture me.

► *Moving*

Every five years, about 30 to 40 percent of American teenagers will move. And the average teenager can expect to move at least once between the ages of 12 and 18.[1]

In the process, kids lose their home, friends, neighbors, neighborhood, community, school, church, classes, teachers, secret places and public hangouts. And they're expected to cope with an avalanche of new things—house, room, school, friends, teachers, neighbors, church and community.

Talk about stress!

Moving is no less traumatic for adults. Our losses and adjustments are just as stressful. However, experience has taught us to take our time adjusting. We don't try to do everything right away. We don't have to become fast friends with the first smile we encounter. We don't have to join every club or organization just to meet people. We shop around and get to know the lay of the land. Then we decide what we're going to do.

But kids don't feel they can afford that kind of time. In four short years, their high school career will end. If they spend too much time getting to know the lay of the land, they will have missed once-in-a-lifetime opportunities.

Sometimes adults encourage this kind of panic by telling kids to get involved early. "Don't mope around feeling sorry for yourself. Get involved. Go out for the track team. Make new friends."

Anxiety about fitting in and being accepted is increased in a new school, church or community. Stress bubbles up and begins to boil over, adding to the normal stress parents are feeling from the move. Like a pressure cooker without a release valve, it threatens to explode.

Ease the pressures and stresses of a move by preparing, learning and taking it easy.

Preparing—Getting ready for a move helps ease the stress and feelings of loss kids experience when they leave one town and move to another. It also makes the transition much easier. Here are ways to prepare:

- Make the losses as gradual as possible. Have a party to say goodbye to friends. At the party, have your teenager collect addresses and hand out post cards addressed to himself or herself at your new address. Keeping in touch with friends through the mail eases the pain of separation. Gradually, the notes and letters will diminish until they're only Christmas cards and an occasional birthday greeting. The transition will be complete.

● Begin packing early. Pack a few things at a time, marking the boxes clearly. This process not only lets you slip gradually into the transition, it makes unpacking a lot easier.

● A move works best if it's a group project. When moving day arrives—whether you move yourself or hire movers—include everyone in the process. Assign tasks. Give specific people responsibility for precious items. And get some picnic food that everyone enjoys.

Learning—Whether it's across town or across the country, your new community is still a different place with different things to see and experience. Learn as much as you can about it before you go.

The more you know about a community, the sooner you can call it home. Make learning about the new place a family activity. Get everyone involved in research and discovery. Have fun talking together about new opportunities, sights and services.

Get to know the historical, political, socioeconomic and cultural climate. Learn about recreation opportunities, churches, services, neighborhoods and attractions in the community.

You can get books, articles and other literature about your new area through a variety of sources, including:

- the local library;
- real estate offices;
- service clubs; and
- the Chamber of Commerce.

The local telephone book contains a wealth of information about the community. Thumb through the Yellow Pages to see what kinds of retail outlets and services are available.

As a family, drive through the community and get a feel for things. Where's the grocery store? the library? the post office? the schools? Get a feel for the kinds of people who

Our New Community

When you're moving to a new community, use this worksheet to learn as much as you can about your new home.

Name of community: ______________________

New address: ______________________

New phone number: ______________________

High school: ______________________

Address: ____________ Phone: ____________

Principal's name: ____________ Mascot: ____________

Middle school/junior high: ______________________

Address: ____________ Phone: ____________

Principal's name: ____________ Mascot: ____________

Elementary school: ______________________

Address: ____________ Phone: ____________

Principal's name: ____________ Mascot: ____________

Closest church of our denomination: ______________________

Address: ____________ Phone: ____________

Pastor: ____________ Youth leader: ____________

Sunday morning worship time: ______________________

Christian education time: ______________________

Youth group time: ______________________

Other information of interest: ______________________

____

continued

Closest library: ______________________________

Closest fast-food restaurant: ______________________________

Closest pharmacy: ______________ Phone: ______________

Closest grocery store: ______________ Hours: ______________

Police phone: ______________________________

Fire phone: ______________________________

Fun things to do in this community:

1. ______________________________

____

2. ______________________________

____

3. ______________________________

____

4. ______________________________

____

live in the community and what life's like.

Taking it easy—Tough as it may be, help your teenager take his or her time fitting in and getting to know people.

Encourage your teenager to take time to consider the impression he or she wants to make and how to make it. While moving can be a cause of distress, it can also be an opportunity to start over.

Did she like her image and reputation at her old school? Would he like to change something about other people's perception of him? Now's the chance. No one has expectations for your teenager to fulfill.

And parents, slow down. Ask yourself what's really important in your new home. Is it really necessary to have every picture hung in every room of the house by the second week?

I've moved three times in the past eight years, and I find the one-room-at-a-time method helpful. We have the movers put the stuff in all the appropriate rooms. Then we close the doors. We make sure the rooms are operable, but the finishing touches have to wait.

First we open the door to room one and begin getting it in shape. When it's finished, we celebrate. Then we start on room two. Little by little the whole place all gets done, and we still have time to talk to each other and enjoy ourselves.

► *Divorce*

Researchers predict about 60 percent of our children will spend at least part of their childhood in a single-parent household. And if projections are correct, the step-families and single-parent families will soon outnumber the "traditional" families in the United States.[2]

Next to death, divorce causes more stress in a family than anything else. Especially for teenagers. Young people who were children when their parents divorced tend to experience these side effects:

- They feel sad and vulnerable.
- They grieve for the loss of the intact family and, often, their lost relationship with their absent parent.

Single-Parent Families

When a divorce or death creates a single-parent family, the results include a number of unique stresses. The resulting feelings include:

Inadequacy—Being the parent of a teenager is tough. Doing it alone is really tough. But it isn't impossible. Sure, there are some things you won't be able to do alone. But there are some things that every parent can't do and that kids will miss—no matter how many parents they have.

Guilt—Guilt can cripple a single parent's effectiveness. Guilt for asking kids to cook their own meals. Guilt for not being able to provide for them financially as you'd like. Guilt because they have only one parent.

It's important to deal with these feelings in a healthy, constructive way. Find support and fellowship of other adults who can share and understand your feelings and support you in your parenting.

Loneliness—A single parent may feel lonely. You're all there is. If there's an emergency, there isn't a spouse to call for help. If there's a problem, you have to handle it yourself.

Loneliness often results from acting out of guilt. Single parents feel lonely because they can't do everything. And the appropriate response is similar to the response to guilt. Make a life for yourself. Develop friendships and activities outside your family. You needn't abandon your kids to do this. Become active in your church or the parent-teacher group. Get to know other parents and make friends.

Feelings of manipulation—Teenagers are among the best manipulators in the world. If they know you're feeling guilty or lonely they may not be above using that to get what they want—"Dad always lets me do this" or "You never do this for me."

It's important not to give into this kind of manipulation. The best answer to statements like these is "What you and your dad decide is between you and your dad. This is what I need." Or "We all do things differently. This is my way."

Be firm, be fair and be yourself. You are the best thing you can give your kids. Don't be manipulated into giving them something less.

- Relationships with the opposite sex and personal commitments create anxiety and are difficult for them.
- They tend to not trust in relationships, feeling they'll be hurt, betrayed or abandoned.
- Girls tend to become involved in dating and sexual relationships earlier.
- Guys tend to be lonely and avoid relationships.[3]

Parents involved in a divorce are often so caught up in their own pain and grief they don't have the sensitivity, time or energy to deal effectively with the stress their kids feel. Yet the children need strong support.

This is a time to get help. The complexities of divorce are simply too complicated to handle alone, especially when kids are involved. If you reach the point where divorce is a reality in your life, find a pastor or counselor who can help you sort out your feelings. And do the same for your kids.

In the meantime, keep in mind these dos and don'ts:

- *Do* make it clear to your kids that the divorce is not their fault. They didn't cause it, and they couldn't have prevented it.
- *Don't* ask or expect your kids to take sides. While your relationship with your spouse has changed, theirs probably hasn't.
- *Do* remember that it's your divorce, not theirs. Their lives go on and their needs remain constant.
- *Don't* try to be supermom or superdad. Get help when you feel you need it. This is a difficult, painful time for you, and there's nothing wrong with asking for help.
- *Do* keep your promises. If you have visitation rights or joint custody, take that commitment seriously. Be there on time and ready to be a parent.
- *Don't* stop being a parent. Your child is still your child. He or she is not your therapist, best friend, confessor or helpmate. Forcing a teenager into one of these roles only increases the stress he or she already feels.
- *Do* assure kids that a failed relationship is not a failed life. Their parents' divorce doesn't reflect on their own ability to sustain a relationship.
- *Don't* forget about your faith. As a family, turn to God and the church as sources of healing and forgiveness.

Stress-Reducers for Blended Families

The stresses visited upon blended families—or step-families—are legion. Here are 10 suggestions for dealing with the three biggest stresses: discipline, resentment and jealousy.

1. Remember that all families with teenagers must deal with issues of discipline, resentment and jealousy regularly—not just blended families. So you're not alone.

2. Share yourself, but don't force yourself on your step-kids. Don't overcompensate or apologize for who you are. Relax. Be yourself around your step-children.

3. Be patient. Trust, respect and admiration take time. It's not fair to expect kids to give you those things just because you're older than they are. Most parents who discipline their children effectively do so in the context of a relationship that has been built over a long period of time.

4. Get help. The complex emotions and problems that come up in step-family relationships are often too difficult to handle alone. Find a step-parent support group in your community. If there aren't any, consider starting one.

5. Present a united front in discipline. Establish firm and fair family rules and guidelines. Make sure everyone in the family knows the rules and what to expect if they're broken. When the rules are broken they are "our" rules, not "my" rules. Level penalties cooly and calmly. Don't take broken rules personally.

6. Be supportive and—as much as possible—friendly with absent parents. You can't take their place, and your step-children need to continue to develop their relationship with their biological parents.

7. Be sensitive about the little things. Honoring last names, privacy, personal space and private property can help create good will.

8. Be supportive. Show up at ball games, school plays, parent/teacher conferences and church functions. A supportive parent does wonders for a teenager's self-esteem.

9. Be honest. Share yourself with your family. Tell the kids how you feel. If you're having a bad time at work, let them know about it. If their table manners drive you crazy, calmly explain your feelings. Your honesty may not change things immediately. But it sets a pattern of openness.

10. Listen. Understanding is the first step in getting along. Instead of fighting about someone's behavior, ask yourself why he or she is acting that way.

● *Do* create a sense of ritual and routine in your family's life. Small things serve as anchors in stormy times.

► Support in Stressful Changes

You may recall that I credited the church with being the one constant—and possibly the thing that saved my sanity—in my early adolescence. Yet I hardly mentioned it as I discussed the various stresses of change.

I don't believe my faith and my church offer magic talismans for dealing with every stress that comes. The scriptures do not contain recipes or formulas for dealing with the specific stresses of being a parent or a teenager in the late 20th century.

Rather, our Christian faith assures us we're not alone in this world. When everything around us seems lost in flux and change, we can still tie our hopes to, and find comfort in, one constant: the God of Abraham, Isaac, Ruth, Naomi, David, Peter and Paul. And the God in whom we hope and trust. Unchanging and unchanged.

The God who brought the children of Israel through the wilderness will bring a teenager through a divorce.

The God who saw Israel through the Babylonian captivity will see me through my move to a new community.

The God who opened Paul's eyes to the love of Christ will open my eyes to the challenges of change.

This God of faithfulness is the same God we worshiped as children and the same God we speak of to our children.

The God who experienced the growing pains of adolescence through his Son, Jesus Christ, stands beside us with comfort, support and guidance.

And it's our faith in this God and our active participation in his church that bring us through whatever change life throws at us.

Endnotes

[1]Eugene C. Roehlkepartain (editor), *The Youth Ministry Resource Book* (Loveland, CO: Group Books, 1988), 24.

[2]Roehlkepartain, *The Youth Ministry Resource Book*, 30.

[3]Roehlkepartain, *The Youth Ministry Resource Book*, 30.

CHAPTER 8

Exercise, Vacations and Other Stress-Reducers

My barber Max runs marathons. He's serious about it, and—knowing I'm a jogger—he talks about it whenever he cuts my hair. He talks about his diet, his training routine, where he runs and how often—and generally more than I want to know about running. And he usually asks me when I'm going to get serious and start running instead of just jogging around the neighborhood. Usually, I tell him "never."

Anyway, I went in a couple of weeks ago for my haircut, took my seat and braced myself for the news from the world of marathon running.

Nothing. He talked about football and baseball and his kids and his church. Not a word about running.

So I asked him, "When's the next big race, Max? How's the training?"

"Not training right now," he said. "You want it off the ears or what?"

"Yeah, off the ears. What do you mean, not training? I thought you marathoners were always training."

He snorted out a laugh. Ah, the ignorance of amateurs. "Nah," he said. "I'm restin'."

I asked him to explain. It seems he'd run in a race the previous weekend and didn't do as well as he thought he should have. He couldn't figure it out. Finally, he took his story to a trainer to get a professional opinion. The trainer took one look at Max's running diary and said: "You're tired, kid. Take a break."

So Max was resting. He wasn't running, jogging, reading about running, thinking about running or talking about running. After two weeks he'd be ready to go back at it—well-rested and ready to train.

●

I think Max's experience says a lot about stress. For most of this book we've talked about getting ourselves into good shape so we can handle stress. We've talked about how to get through it, tough it out, fight it and win. And usually, these things work.

But they can't and won't work always and everywhere. Sometimes you can't fight. Sometimes you have to flee—run away from the stress and the things that are causing it.

In this chapter, we'll look at different, healthy ways to run away.

► *Avoiding Stress Before It Comes*

Often we make decisions that put us in stressful situations. We accept responsibilities we're not good at. We agree to do things we don't want to do. We get into situations that offer little reward. In short, we add to the stress in our lives when we really don't need to.

Of course, sometimes we add to our own stress knowingly because something's important to us. We may agree to coach soccer because we enjoy sports and want to be with kids. But that's a different matter. In this chapter, we're concerned with stresses we walk into without really meaning to.

A lot of the stress in our lives can be avoided if we're willing to make the effort. Here are three simple ways to avoid stressful situations without adding other kinds of stress to your life.

Go around. As he got older, my father-in-law hated to drive on freeways. He felt freeways were too fast, and he didn't have the skills to handle driving on them.

So he went around—drove on small streets, stopping for traffic lights and stop signs. It would drive anyone else crazy. But he could handle it.

If you know in advance something will stress you out,

go around it. Find ways to do what needs to be done without doing something that will obviously cause you stress.

Cooking something new drives my wife crazy. The heat, the work, the mess, the worry—they just stress her out. So she developed what she calls "my meals." These are 10 basic meals she prepares. Between her 10 and my five, we rarely get bored. And if we do, there's always peanut butter and jelly in the cabinet.

Go through. Many years ago, I went to the Indianapolis 500. With just a couple of laps to go, there was a huge, smoking wreck right in front of me. The three lead cars were involved. Pieces of the cars were strewn all over the track. Smoke obstructed everyone's view. The three drivers were seen running out of the smoke.

Within seconds of the crash, the fourth car came around the turn at well over 100 mph. We held our breath as he entered the cloud of smoke, expecting to hear the sound of his car crashing into another. But a few seconds later we saw him speed through to win the race.

That night, reporters asked the winner how he managed to maneuver his car through all the smoke and mess so fast. "I closed my eyes," he said.

Sometimes the best way to avoid a stressful situation is to forge ahead and bust through as quickly as possible. It's like putting out a candle with your fingers or ripping off a Band-Aid. The trick is to do it so quickly that you don't have time to feel it.

The same principle often holds true for parenting. When the stress of parenting seems overwhelming, forge ahead. Close your eyes and keep going. Do it quickly so you don't feel the pain. Often, the *act* of parenting will get you through the *stress* of parenting.

Your teenager's teacher calls and wants you to come in for a conference. It has to be bad news or the teacher wouldn't call. Your first reaction: Make an excuse why you can't possibly come this week. (Flight.) Second reaction: What's the matter with this teacher? Can't he handle my kid? Can't she do her job? (Fight.)

Appropriate reaction: Act!

No matter how much you hate these meetings, deal

with the problem immediately. "I'll be there in an hour." You may be surprised to learn the teacher hates these meetings as much as you do. Finding out you are anxious and willing to deal with the problem quickly will make the meeting go a lot smoother.

Just close your eyes and plunge ahead.

Stay away. Remember the old doctor joke?

Patient: Doctor, it hurts when I do this.

Doctor: Well, don't do that!

Sometimes the best way to avoid stress is to stay away from things that cause it. Does cooking stress you out? Don't cook. Do meetings drive you crazy? Don't go. Are you all thumbs when it comes to fixing things? Don't fix things. Do you feel like a fool when you dance? Don't dance.

It really is that simple.

Just say no!

I know. It isn't always easy to say no, is it? Okay, here are some ways to help you out. I've found they never fail.

- Blame someone else. "Sorry, I'd love to do that, but I've made a promise to my kids." Be sure what you're saying is true.
- Put it off. Never carry your calendar with you. Then you can say, "I'll have to check my calendar and let you know." That gives you time to come up with a legitimate excuse for saying no.
- Suggest someone else. "I'm afraid I can't help you on that one. But I know just the person you should call . . ."
- Be honest, but be funny. "Mary, to be honest, that kind of thing just drives me out of my gourd. I'd rather climb a cactus in the buff than have to go through something like that. There must be something else I can do that will leave me with my sanity."

More important than saying no to other people, however, is saying no to yourself. And you can't make up excuses for yourself. You just have to say it: No.

Is your weight causing you stress? Say no to dessert.

Are arguments stressing your family? Say no to arguing and bickering.

Is your overbooked schedule giving you stress? Say no to other commitments.

When Jesus approached the pool at Bethesda, he was surrounded by a multitude of sick and lame people. Yet he healed only the one person (John 5). Just that one guy, and then he left. For whatever reason, he said no to the others.

Saying no is not always easy and it doesn't always please the people around us. But if we are to deal effectively with our own stress, we must learn to say it.

► *Exercising to Relieve Stress*

Exercise helps us deal with stress by creating a healthy outlet for our body's stress responses. As a side effect, we get to look and feel better about ourselves.

A couple of weeks ago I lost my checkbook.

No problem, I said to myself. I must've left it at my office. I remember writing a check at my desk.

So I drove over to the office. No checkbook.

Hmmm. Well, I must've missed it when I looked on the dresser. I'll go back and look again. Drove back. Went upstairs. No checkbook.

The stress started building. Two hours—and several commutes between home and work—later I'd looked every place it could possibly be. House, office, both cars.

Panic. I called every place I'd been in the past three days.

Nothing. No checkbook. Absolute, maximum panic! Total stress!

I could feel the tenseness in my body. My heart beat faster, and I was reacting angrily to people and things around me. I felt an overwhelming need to *do* something.

So I went to work out. Stationary bike. Weight machines. Out of breath. Sweating like a convict in an August courthouse. Cool shower. Totally exhausted, I returned home.

It sure seems nice to drive a clean car for a change, I thought to myself. I should clean it more often. All those hamburger wrappers and candy bar papers and . . .

That's it! I had cleaned out the car—just scooped up all the stuff and dumped it in the garbage!

I raced home, ran to the garbage can and dumped it on the grass.

Bingo! There was the checkbook. It had been lying on the car seat when I dumped everything in the trash. Now, how do I explain all those coffee grounds and grease stains on my checks?

Through that checkbook episode, I could feel the natural stress reaction happening. My breathing, my pulse, my nerves—everything was ready to fight or flee.

Unfortunately, fighting or fleeing wouldn't help me find my checkbook. Thinking was the only thing that could do that. But I couldn't think. My body's reaction to the stress had taken over.

When parents are dealing with the stress of raising a teenager, acting out the instinct to fight or flee rarely helps. But sometimes our body screams so loudly for that kind of reaction, it's almost impossible not to give in. Thinking goes out the window. Acting steps in.

Trouble results.

We can't ignore our bodies when they speak so loudly. But we can channel that stress into something useful and helpful. Exercise is one of the best ways to relieve this stress.

Choosing your exercise routine—As you choose an exercise program, it's important to find one that fits you and your needs. Check with your doctor and someone trained in fitness. And ask yourself some questions to make your program work for you:

- How much can I spend? Some programs are expensive. Others cost next to nothing. Do I want to spend a lot of money on something that may turn out to be boring and silly?
- Can I do a particular exercise three times a week without boring myself to death or killing myself physically? Is the exercise convenient enough so excuses won't keep me from doing it?
- Will I exercise alone? Or is there someone I can exercise with regularly? Handball or racquetball require a partner. Do I have a partner I can count on?
- Am I a morning person, day person or evening person? *When* you feel like exercising may affect what kind of exercise you do. If you have to be at work at 7 a.m. you probably will need to exercise in the evening.

- How disciplined am I? Am I a self-starter, or will I need someone or something to get me started when it's time to do the work?
- Will a particular exercise benefit my whole body? A well-rounded exercise program exercises the whole body. If your choice doesn't, combine it with something else. For example, ride the stationary bicycle for 20 minutes, then do some sit-ups and push-ups.
- Will the exercise be aerobic? Make sure your routine makes your heart beat at your "target heart rate" for 20 to 30 minutes, three times per week. (Your doctor can tell you what that rate is.) This will also cause deep breathing.
- Does my routine build my strength? After a couple of weeks you should be able to tell a difference in how you feel. You should feel better. Your muscle tone should be improving. If it isn't, ask your doctor or trainer for help.
- Does the routine include flexibility exercises? Flexibility keeps you from pulling muscles and getting sore after everyday tasks, such as weeding the garden and washing the car.

Exercising with your family—For many of us, exercise is a personal, private activity. It gets us away from the stresses of work and family. But exercise can also be a great family activity. It can help reduce family stress while letting you have fun together.

Saying things like, "Why don't you kids get out from in front of that television and get some exercise?" is never as effective as, "Let's take a walk together."

Walking, bicycling and jogging are often more fun when done with someone. Why not make that someone a family member? You'll be surprised how much talking gets done on a 3-mile walk or a 2-mile jog.

Many activities require a partner—handball, racquetball, tennis, golf. Invite your spouse or your teenager to be that partner. Take up a new exercise together.

► *Playing—Just for the Fun of It!*

Don't you wish that, just once, you could do something without having a goal you were supposed to reach? Wouldn't it be nice to do something that had no objective, no reward—except the simple joy of doing it?

Well, play!

Play is something you do for fun. There's no point. That's why it relieves stress. When you play, you forget stress, ignore its causes, don't worry about it.

Try it. It's fun.

When the Ark of God was brought into the city of Jerusalem, David, his family and all of Israel were ecstatic. They danced and played and had a grand old time.

No reason. No goal. They just felt like doing it. In 2 Samuel we're told David took off his robe and celebrated by dancing with all his might before the Lord.

Of course, his wife wasn't all that thrilled. What would people think? Their king acting like a commoner—a normal person. It was, well, vulgar. He ought to be more dignified, more kinglike.

But I think David had the right idea. Make merry before the Lord. Play. Dance. Have fun. Life is stressful enough without worrying about what the neighbors will think if we're reckless enough to have a good time.

As adults, we lose this wonderful release. We get too dignified, too serious, too busy. We don't play. We don't pretend. We don't act spontaneously.

It wouldn't hurt us to try it once in a while. Here's what I think of when I think of play.

Play involves pretend. How long has it been since you pretended—since you forgot your troubles and immersed yourself in another place, another time, another personality that existed only in your head?

Yeah. I thought so.

So give it a try!

- Build a sand castle and then turn yourself into a monster that destroys it.
- Pretend you're a cop and tail someone. I don't care who, just try it.
- Be a private eye and solve a murder. You can buy games and books that let you do just that.

Play involves exploration. It really is amazing how you'll leave behind stress at the old place while you explore a new one!

Take the family to a different town or city and explore it just to see what you can see. Find some neat stuff. Walk around and look for those little stores and shops you never see when you're driving.

Or take the scenic route somewhere. Stop at the mom-and-pop grocery and try out a different kind of soft drink.

Play is rarely competitive. I hear adults say, "I play! Why just the other night I played one-on-one at the park with the guys!"

That's not play—not really! It's work disguised as play! You keep score. You worry about your form and ability.

Play is done for the pure joy of doing it. Look at the difference:

Work	Play
Swinging on a trapeze	Swinging on a vine
Canoeing down a river	Tubing down a creek
Fishing for bass with an expensive rod and reel	Fishing with a cane pole and night crawlers

See the difference? Work tries to accomplish something. Play is for the pure joy of doing it. And when you lose yourself in the joy of doing an activity, stress disappears.

Play is often silly. Have a snowball fight. Or a water balloon fight. Throw marshmallows at your kids. Hide a whoopee cushion on the couch.

Squirt your spouse with the hose. Build a snow dog instead of a snow man. Finger-paint. Pretend you're British and talk with an accent all day.

Eat a whole box of ice cream sandwiches. Roll down a hill in the grass. Swing on the swings at the park. Go down the slide. Ride the merry-go-round.

Just have fun!

► *Taking Stress-Free Vacations*

Several years ago, on the Saturday before Easter, I was ready to collapse. (Lent and Advent are stressful times for ministers.) I was expressing to my wife just how I felt when she said, "Let's take a vacation."

"That vacation was great! Let's go again next year!"

"Yeah, sure. Just take off and go," I retorted sarcastically.

"Sure," she said, as though it was the most normal thing in the world. "The kids are off school next week. You get three weeks of vacation."

"Where could we go? We're broke." I had her there. We couldn't afford to go anyplace.

"Florida," she said.

"Florida?"

"Sure, Florida. We'll drive down. Put the gas on the credit card, get a cheap room, lay on the beach and eat sandwiches and oranges all week."

This was a ridiculous whim. Obviously, she hadn't thought things out. "Do you realize how much that would cost us? Besides, it's spring break! I don't want to be in Florida over spring break."

As it turned out, she knew exactly how much it would cost. She'd even found a beach condo that was less expensive than a motel. The beach was on the Gulf Coast, away from the crowds. And it was still available. She'd done her homework.

So I called the senior minister and arranged to be gone. The next day I came home after our Easter services and went to bed—while my wife and the kids packed the station wagon. At 6 p.m. she woke me up. The car was packed, the kids were in their pajamas. We started driving and arrived at noon the next day.

For five glorious days I sat on the beach getting sunburned and reading detective novels while the kids played in the surf. Breakfast was oranges and doughnuts in the room. Lunch was a bologna sandwich and a diet soda on the beach. Around 5 p.m. we'd get cleaned up and go out for dinner. Someplace reasonable—pizza or burgers.

Then a round of miniature golf or just a walk on the beach watching the sunset. We'd go to bed early and be up early the next day to do the same thing. Relaxing is a dirty job, but someone has to do it.

We took two days to drive back to Ohio. When we arrived we were all refreshed, rested, tanned and ready to tackle our lives again.

I think it was the best vacation I've ever had. And we

spent all of a day and a half planning it. Sometimes things just work out right.

And sometimes they don't. Our family has also experienced what my kids still remember as "The Vacation From Hell." Everything went wrong. The weather, the car, the accommodations, the entertainment, the money. A total bust. I arrived at home more stressed than when I left.

Vacations can help us get away from stress or they can create their own stress for us. Having experienced the best and worst that vacations have to offer, I think I've learned about how to make them work. Here's what I've learned.

Do something you can afford. When my kids were little, we developed a rule about money on vacations. It goes something like this—on vacation you have two choices:

- You can spend the time being happy about what you can afford to do.
- Or you can spend it being unhappy about what you can't afford to do.

Choose whichever one you like. But if you take number two, keep it to yourself.

If you have to worry about money the whole time you're on vacation, you won't have a good time. You'll just cause yourself more stress.

So plan a vacation budget, then create a vacation that fits it. I've included a "Vacation Budget Worksheet" on page 126. Use it to decide exactly how much money you can spend and what you'll spend it on.

Have minimal expectations. One reason vacations so often disappoint us is we expect so much from them.

Our Florida vacation worked so well partly because we did it on the spur of the moment. We didn't have time to build up a lot of expectations about what we'd do. Basically, we were going to relax. We'd do whatever it took to accomplish that one task. That's all.

This doesn't mean you can't look forward to your vacation. It does mean you shouldn't try to plan and control every moment of your time. Leave lots of free time and wait-and-see time.

A friend of mine keeps his teenagers' expectations in line by saying: "This is your mother's and my vacation too.

We're planning to spend a part of each day relaxing. We'll do one major thing you kids choose each day. That's a promise. But don't bug us about it. We'll do it. Trust us."

Get away from home. The root word of vacation is "vacate"—leave, go away, remove yourselves from the premises.

Stay-at-home-and-do-fun-things-around-here vacations never work. At home there's all that stuff staring you in the face, saying, "Do me! Do me!" And since no one else will do it, you do.

That's not a vacation. Get away!

Do the opposite of what you do in your work. Generally, people like to do on vacation what they don't get to do at other times. In my work, I spend a lot of time solving problems and making decisions. So I try to create vacations where I don't have to solve any problems. And the heaviest decision I have to make is whether to have coffee or tea with breakfast.

If you do physical labor for a living, you may want to lie around on vacation. But if you have a sedentary job, you may want to do something active, such as hiking or skiing. If you're a cab driver, you won't relax by spending your vacation behind the wheel. If you're a custodian, you'll probably want room service.

Remember, the point of a vacation is to get away from stress—not to experience it in a different location.

Time vacations to fit your lifestyle. You're the only one who knows when you need a break. Some people need one long vacation once a year. Others need several small vacations spread throughout the year.

When I was in college, I discovered the quarter system worked well for me. I'd go hard for three months, then take a week off. I still try to do this whenever I can.

I have a friend, though, who takes all three of her weeks together, goes to a cabin in the mountains and spends the whole time fishing and reading. She says she can't really unwind in only one week.

Take everyone's needs into consideration. If you want your vacation to be successful and stress-free, bring everyone into the planning. Find out what each person wants

Vacation Budget Worksheet

Use this worksheet to plan your next vacation. Use the sheet for several options so you can discover the best way to meet your family's needs without busting your budget and adding to your stress.

Housing

(Cost for whole vacation)

Cabin or condominium: $ ________

RV (rent): $ ________

House (rent): $ ________

Camper hookup: $ ________

Bed and breakfast: $ ________

Motel or hotel: $ ________

Cottage: $ ________

Other: ____________ $ ________

1. Total for housing: $ ________

Transportation

(Miles round trip: ____________)

Auto (at 20 cents/mile): $ ________

Plane: $ ________

Train: $ ________

Other: ____________ $ ________

2. Total for transportation: $ ________

Entertainment and Recreation

Options	***Cost***
____________________________	$ ________
____________________________	$ ________
____________________________	$ ________
____________________________	$ ________

3. Total for entertainment and recreation: $ ________

continued

Meals and Snacks

_______ (number) of breakfasts at $ _________ each: $ _________

_______ (number) of lunches at $ _________ each: $ _________

_______ (number) of dinners at $ _________ each: $ _________

_______ (number) of snacks at $ _________ each: $ _________

4. Total cost for food: $ _________

Purchases Before the Trip

(clothes, toys, suntan oil)

Items	*Cost*
_________________________	$ _________
_________________________	$ _________
_________________________	$ _________

5. Total for purchases before the trip: $ _________

Total Vacation Cost
(add totals from lines 1 through 5): $ _________

and needs from a vacation. Then try to plan at least a little of that into the trip.

Also, find out what each person absolutely wants to avoid, and see if there's a way to avoid it. If not, be willing to make some trade-offs.

For instance, my wife hates to ride long distances in the car. But she also loves Florida—about 18 hours away. We can't afford to fly. So what do we do?

Well, first we make clear there has to be a trade-off. If you want to go to Florida, you have to spend 18 hours in the car. There's no way around it. But you don't have to spend all those hours at one stretch. We can break up the trip into two days. Or we can drive overnight, and she can sleep while I drive. I enjoy driving and listening to the radio while everyone else sleeps. I like the quiet and the light traffic late at night.

The kids like to be entertained. They like to *do* stuff. I like to do nothing. So we compromise. We go someplace where they can do stuff while I do nothing.

Before you plan the vacation, make everyone in the family complete the following statements:

- On this vacation I want/need to . . .
- I definitely don't want to . . .
- To get to do what I want and avoid what I don't want on this vacation, I'm willing to . . .

Pull together everyone's responses and plan together to meet everyone's needs.

Decide you're going to have a good vacation. When I was a kid, my mother used to say: "Rain never ruins a picnic. Disappointment ruins picnics."

Her logic applies to vacations too. If I have decided to enjoy my time off with my family, no amount of rain will keep me from doing that. If, on the other hand, I decide the only way I can be happy is to spend thousands of dollars at the world's biggest amusement park on a bright, sunshiny day where the temperature never goes above 75 degrees and the crowds are small . . . well, I'll probably be unhappy.

Be flexible.

Solve problems as they come up.

Accept the inevitable.

Decide to be happy.

Do these things and, chances are, your vacation will be about as fun and stress-free as they get.

► Taking Parent Escapes

I not only love my kids, I like them. I enjoy their company, and I usually have a good time when I'm with them. But sometimes we need to get away from our kids and renew our relationships with our spouses.

So once in a while, my wife and I leave our kids with friends or relatives and take off by ourselves.

Sometimes it's a weekend. Sometimes it's a whole week. Sometimes, it's just an overnight escape at a nice hotel.

It's always a great break. We get away from the stress of working and parenting, even if only for a brief time. We can do what we want to do when we want to do it. We don't have to worry about the kids being bored or tired or anxious to get home. We can just take care of ourselves for a while.

How can you add these kinds of trips to your vacation time? Easy. Conventions. Continuing education trips. Meetings. Long weekends. Minor holidays. Any excuse will do.

For this kind of "parent time out" to work, we have several things in place:

● First, Jean and I do it as part of our regular mom-and-dad time pattern. That is, we've raised our kids to understand that—from time to time—Mom and Dad need to be alone together. To solve problems, to visit, to talk, to make love. It doesn't really matter what we do; it's our private time, and we can do with it what we please.

● Second, we have a network of friends and relatives who'll look after each other's kids. If your kids are teenagers, they may like the idea of spending the night with a friend while you get away from home yourselves.

If someone is coming to be with your teenagers while you're gone, make sure your kids understand why this arrangement is necessary. It's not that you don't trust them;

sometimes an adult is really handy to have around in case of an emergency.

Let your kids and the adult chaperone know the rules and expectations while you're gone. Avoid the word "babysitter" at all costs.

● Third, we don't do it very often. Probably not more than once a year. And our kids know we aren't trying to get away from them so much as we are trying to get with each other. They realize we're usually better parents when we get back from one of these trips.

● Fourth, we don't substitute these trips for family vacations. We manage to add them on. We don't expect the kids to give up their vacation so we can take one without them.

► *Giving Kids Time Out*

Kids go at life hard and fast. Adults tend to approach life like a marathon; kids tend to approach it like a 100-yard dash.

So they need shorter, more frequent breaks than adults do.

And let's face it, they need breaks from us too.

Some youth groups and organizations offer these kinds of opportunities through campouts, retreats, trips, lock-ins and other getaways. Help out from time to time, but respect your kids' needs to get away from you and find themselves in their own environment. Encourage them to get away from time to time, make new friends and hear input from different adults you trust.

But sometimes even this isn't enough. Sometimes, they need to get away for just an hour or so. And to do that they need their own space and time.

Not every household can provide a private room for every person. But there can be personal space for each person that is respected by all others in the family. Respect that space:

- Knock before you enter someone's room.
- Don't paw through your teenager's stuff.
- Give your teenager a little private time when he or

she seems to need it.

● Allow your teenager his or her own escapes—music, activities, moods. Sometimes these things that drive us crazy are important escapes.

And all of us need to escape a little from time to time.

► *Retreating for Renewal*

Sometimes we think we can handle the stresses of daily life without taking breaks or taking care of ourselves. But we're only kidding ourselves. Everyone needs a break—including Jesus. In Mark 6:30-32, we read:

> The apostles returned to Jesus, and told him all that they had done and taught. And he said to them, "Come away by yourselves to a lonely place, and rest a while." For many were coming and going, and they had no leisure even to eat. And they went away in the boat to a lonely place by themselves.

Even Jesus and the apostles needed to get away from the stresses of their ministries from time to time. They did it by getting in a boat and going away to a "lonely place."

Today, we call it a retreat. Or a vacation. Or private time.

Whatever we call it, it works.

Jesus knew it.

And we need to remember it too.

CHAPTER 9

Getting Perspective

When my son, Ben, was about 4 years old, he went through a phase of calling me by my first name. "Hey, Dean, I like this book." "Dean, can I go with you?"

Dean this and Dean that.

Some folks at the church where I worked thought it was scandalous. They were sure he was being disrespectful. They thought, and said, I should do something about this situation—and pronto—before it got out of hand.

So I looked up the word "dad." I discovered its origin is a mystery. Either it comes from baby talk or from Old English. In Old English the word is "daud" or "daudy"—which means a small piece broken off of a larger whole.

Oh, great . . .

That didn't really work. So I looked up my name. It can mean a number of things. Old English: from the valley. Latin: leader of 10. Modern English: teacher.

Well, any of those is better than a "daud" or "daudy."

So I wrote a humorous little piece for the church newsletter about my investigation. And as you can imagine, it solved nothing. Some people thought it was scandalous. Others still thought it was cute. Others figured Ben was my wife's son by an unknown previous marriage or something.

I just continued to laugh it off or ignore it. About a month later, Ben started calling me Dad again. And everyone was happy.

I think of the "First Name Episode" often when things get tough—how I was able to deal with a situation that might have been really stressful without suffering that first ounce of stress.

Since then, I've printed on cards five principles I learned from that incident and hung them above my writing table. And as often as I can, I try to use them to head off stress before it happens.

► *Principle #1: Remember What's Really Important*

Just because Ben was calling me Dean didn't mean his feelings toward me had changed. We still hugged and kissed. He jumped onto my lap the instant I sat down. That was the important stuff to me. As long as he did those things he could call me Elmer Fudd and I wouldn't care.

When something is causing stress, think: Is this thing worth all the worry and stress I'm putting myself through for it? Is it worth the time and energy I'm giving to it?

Is it a problem to be solved, a crisis to be handled or a tragedy to be endured? Decide which and treat it accordingly.

► *Principle #2: Keep Your Sense of Humor*

When I was trying to defuse the situation with Ben, I didn't think for a minute that Dad really means "a small piece broken off of a larger whole." But I thought it was funny. So I used it in the newsletter.

Let's face it. Kids say and do stuff that's funny. I say and do stuff that's funny . . . sometimes when I don't really mean to.

My dad was always funny when he got mad at us kids. He'd get all flustered and say things that were meant to be threatening. But they'd come out, well, funny. It was nearly impossible not to laugh. Even for him.

Once when I was about 14, I was bickering with my younger siblings in the back of the station wagon for most of a three-hour trip to my grandparents'. About the 15th time he told us to stop arguing, he got mad—and said something funny.

We all laughed.

"That's it!" he yelled. "Laugh! Well, in about two minutes, I'm going to pull over and take off my belt. And *then* you'll laugh."

Long pause. Broad smile.

"Because my pants will probably fall down!"

The image of my father chasing us around the car in his boxer shorts, his belt in one hand and his trousers in the other was too much. We exploded in laughter. The rest of the trip passed without arguing. There was, however, quite a bit of giggling.

The minute we forget how to laugh at the funny things we and our kids do, we become candidates for stress overload.

► *Principle #3: Be Reasonable*

How had Ben picked up his first-name habit? After thinking about it for a while, I realized he'd learned it at church socials, after worship and wherever there was a big crowd.

During those times, dozens of kids would call out, "Dad!" or "Hey Dad!" Ben discovered that, mostly, I'd just blank out all the "Hey, Dads!" I heard, and he wasn't getting through. He also discovered I noticed when someone said, "Hey, Dean!"

Well, if it was good enough for adults, it was good enough for him. He wanted to get my attention when he spoke. And it worked.

In the heat of pressure, it's easy to expect too much from ourselves and others. That's why we need to ask ourselves the question we asked so often as children: "Why?"

Why am I doing this?

Why do I expect this or that of my kids or my spouse or my job?

Why are they doing what they're doing?

Why do they act the way they do?

Discovering the reasons behind what people do and why things are going the way they are often reduces the stress on us.

The car won't start. (Stress) Why? It's out of gas. (Solution to the problem. End of stress.)

The kids are bickering and fighting. (Stress) Why? They're tired and don't feel well. (Solution to the problem. End of stress.)

When we let our feelings rule our behavior, we often open ourselves to stresses we could—with a little thought—avoid. Feelings should inform our behavior, not rule it.

I sometimes feel angry. If I act out that anger by screaming and throwing things, I'll probably just increase the stress for everyone, including myself. But I can avoid much of this stress if I can manage to say to myself: "Hmmm. I'm feeling angry. I think I'll take a walk and decide what to do about it."

► *Principle #4: Be Yourself*

I want people to like me. I want to please people and have them admire the things I do. But I will not parent my children with the goal of pleasing other adults. I will raise my children the way I've determined is helpful for them and me. That's why I handled the first-name incident the way I did. It fit me.

There are yelling families. And there are non-yelling families.

There are neat households. And there are messy households.

There are emotional, hugging, kissing parents. And there are quiet, dignified, supportive parents.

There are conservative, liberal, Southern, Northern, creative, productive, modern, old-fashioned, rich, poor and every other kind of people in the world.

And most of them have families.

Amazingly, children grow up in these diverse families. And the vast majority of them turn out to be happy, productive, well-adjusted adults.

So stop worrying. Be yourself.

I always figured that Atticus Finch, in *To Kill A Mockingbird*, was the perfect father. Or maybe John Walton in *The Waltons*.

But I'm not Atticus Finch, and I'm not John Walton. And I don't want to be. They weren't real. They were made-up. No wonder they were perfect!

I'm not made-up. I'm a real, live, flesh-and-blood guy with kids. And that's what my kids need: a real parent.

Kids need real adults in their lives. Try to be a hero—supermom or superdad—and your kids will see through the pretense in about five seconds. Be the best parent you can be. But be you.

Be honest about who you are. That's the way God made you. If you're tired, say so. If you're bored, share that. If you're in a bad mood, warn your family. If you have a success, celebrate it.

Be yourself. Who you are is God's gift to you—and your family.

► *Principle #5: Be Faithful*

This is the last card that hangs above my writing table. It is, I think, the most important of the bunch. That's because it incorporates and transcends all the rest.

Moses was probably one of the most stressed-out people who ever lived. First, he was raised an orphan. Even if it was in Pharaoh's palace, he was an outsider. And that's got to be stressful.

Then he found out he was a Hebrew. The Hebrews were slaves. They were the lowest of the lower classes—beasts of burden and nothing more. And Moses had been raised as royalty, the most privileged class. It had to be stressful to learn that.

He killed a guard and fled into the desert. We've already talked about the stress of moving. Not to mention the stress he must have felt for killing someone.

Finally, Moses got married, settled down, raised sheep and seemed to be living a normal life. And the next thing you know, God sends him back to Egypt to face down Pharaoh.

Then there's the plague business and the long exodus out of Egypt and the children of Israel harping and complaining and backsliding every time the wind changed. It's a wonder the guy didn't go completely bonkers.

You might think Moses had great inner strength to handle all that stress. But in reality, he wasn't very good at it.

After killing a soldier in anger, Moses ran for his life.

He stammered around when God told him to go to Egypt. Finally God had to send Aaron to help him.

He got mad and broke the Ten Commandments. All of them!

He got mad and struck the rock to produce water.

All in all, Moses didn't handle stress real well.

So how did he do it? How did he manage to accomplish so much when he was such a (admit it) normal person?

The answer, I think, is Moses had the strength of faith. It was his faith that brought him through—not his character.

And it's faith that will ultimately bring us through our stresses as well.

Moses' faith was a gift from God. He responded to the gift in a way that brought him through. What did God give him? How did Moses respond? And how can the story of Moses help us handle the stresses we face?

God gave Moses power. Moses didn't have a good self-image. He certainly didn't have much confidence in his ability to do God's work. But God gave him sufficient power to turn a staff into a serpent and to bring down plagues on Egypt. That wasn't Moses's power; it was God's! Moses was the instrument of God's work.

Likewise, God doesn't call us to do things we can't handle. He gives us gifts and talents, and he expects us to use them in his service.

If we rely solely on our own strength, we'll bring upon ourselves more stress than we can handle. No one is born with the ability to be perfectly empathetic and helpful in every situation. No one has all the answers. Trying to handle all this stuff alone will eventually break us.

But if we open ourselves to God's power and presence, and if we let God work within and through us, we stand a much better chance of being winners. Not only as parents, but as human beings.

God gave Moses the law. God didn't tell Moses to form a committee and come up with some general behavioral guidelines. No, he gave him the law. And that law is the law of love. "You shall love the Lord your God . . . and your neighbor . . ." is how Jesus summarized it (Matthew 19:18-19). The Ten Commandments and all the other Old Testament laws are based on this concept. Jesus reinterpreted the Old Testament laws into a broader, gentler rule for living. And each day, we have to interpret this rule for our own lives.

Even so, the law of love can transcend the problems and stresses we face. It can relieve us of the stress of always having to wonder if we're doing what is pleasing to God. We need only ask: "Is this the loving thing? Is this what Jesus would have us do?"

God gave Moses a calling. Moses was sent to do a job. He was to lead the children of Israel out of bondage. That was it.

In the same way, God calls each of us to a similar task. Children, our children, are in danger of being enslaved. To selfishness. To pride. To convenience. To drugs. To greed. To alcohol.

And we, like Moses, are called to *lead* our children out of this bondage. Not to push them out or threaten them out or bully them out or beat them out. To *lead* them out.

By our example. With discipline and guidance. And with love.

If we tend to this task, our lives will be filled with purpose and meaning. And the stress the task brings to us will be stress we can handle.

God gave Moses time. Moses was already getting old by the time God called him at the burning bush. Acts 7:20-32 reports that Moses spent 40 years learning and growing in the Pharoah's house. Then he fled to Midian where he spent another 40 years tending sheep.

We may wonder why God waited so long to call Moses into his service. But maybe that time was a gift to Moses—an opportunity to learn and build himself into the kind of strong, faithful leader that would be required to lead Israel out of Egypt.

Time is the greatest gift God gives to us. It has a great way of helping us handle our stress.

As a parent, I know I have time to mold and shape my children. I have time to make mistakes and correct them. I have time to build relationships and share experiences. Not enough time to waste, mind you. But enough time to do a thorough job if I use the time well.

Moses responded with faith and obedience. Moses believed there was a God. Moses even believed in God.

Those two things alone wouldn't have made much difference if he hadn't acted on them. But Moses risked. He trusted God. He put himself and his people in God's hands.

People of faith encounter stress because of their beliefs.

But what's the alternative? To be a person without faith? To believe, but not act on our beliefs? To let life happen to us?

Those alternatives lead to more stress than any person can handle.

The Bible tells us the stresses of faith are rewarded. God brings us through them stronger—better than we were before.

God has given us a special resource for handling, getting through and even growing in the midst of the stresses we face. That resource is faith—an affirming, uplifting, positive faith in a loving, forgiving God.

That faith—without doubt—will see us through.

AFTERWORD

An Adventure Without a Map

A couple of years ago, another youth counselor and I took eight senior highers on a canoe trip in the Quetico Provincial Park in Ontario, Canada. The outfitters fixed us up with everything we needed for a seven-day trip—canoes, packs, food, sleeping bags, tents, paddles, life jackets, compasses and maps.

What they didn't fix us up with was the ability to read the maps.

So there we were—four days out—paddling along the bank of this huge lake, looking for the place where the map said we were supposed to portage about a quarter of a mile to another lake.

No portage was visible.

Back and forth along the bank. Looking for a sign—anything that would hint we could cross to the other lake.

But nothing.

So I refolded the map to try again. It's got to be here somewhere, I figured. Then I looked at the bottom of the map. It said something like this: "Geological survey map. Not intended for navigational purposes."

Oh, wonderful.

I shared this bit of information with the other counselor, and we both just sort of looked at each other and shook our heads. Now what?

One of the guys made a suggestion: Let's get out of the

canoes and hike up and down the bank looking for any sign of human beings having portaged here in the past couple weeks.

It was better than being lost, so we did it.

We split up and started up and down the shore. About 20 minutes later I heard a loud whistle. My group turned around and headed for the sound. When we reached the other party, the other counselor was grinning broadly.

"Found it," was all he said as he pointed to an almost invisible break in the trees.

"Wow," I said, "That was some kind of tracking. I never would've seen it. How'd you do it?"

He reached in his pocket and pulled out a small piece of paper—a chewing gum wrapper. On it was scribbled in pencil, "portage here." It had been stuck to a rock with a well-chewed piece of gum.

We stuck it back on the rock and went merrily on our way, grunting and groaning under the weight of the canoes and equipment.

●

This book is like that piece of chewing gum wrapper. It's placed here by someone who has gone before you and wants to help you find a clear path.

But, it can't carry the load for you. It can't take away the stress of parenting a teenager. You'll have to do some grunting and groaning on your own.

What it can do is help point out the path of least resistance.

I offer it with my prayers and best wishes.

Parenting a teenager can be stressful. But it can also be a wonderful and amazing adventure. It's up to you which one it turns out to be.

Vaya con Dios.

Go with God.

Practical Resources for Parents of Teenagers

TALK TRIGGERS

by Thom and Joani Schultz

Choose from over 200 easy-to-use discussion-starting questions to help you and your teenagers spark meaningful and fun conversation.

Your family will improve communication, express themselves, learn about each other and examine faith when you ask each other these zany, insightful, faith-building questions such as . . . "Would you take a bath with thousands of leeches for $5,000?"

Order this book for great conversations at meals, in the car or instead of television. Have fun—while you and your teenager grow closer to each other—and to God.

Family Tree ISBN 0-931529-91-3 160 pages $4.95

FUN DEVOTIONS FOR PARENTS AND TEENAGERS

by James Kochenburger

Now you and your teenagers can have active, fun devotional times together. You'll get 52 ready-to-use devotions on different topics including . . .

- Dating
- Family goals
- Failure
- Church
- Communication
- Financial planning
- Sibling rivalry
- Mutual respect, and more

These easy-to-use devotions can be led by either you or your teenager. Help your family grow closer and strengthen your commitment to God with **Fun Devotions for Parents and Teenagers**.

Family Tree ISBN 1-55945-016-9 $9.95

HELPING YOUR TEENAGER COPE WITH PEER PRESSURE

by Len Kageler

Discover how you can help guide your teenager through the turmoil of peer pressure. You'll learn how to:

- Respond when your teenager faces pressure
- Improve communication with your young person
- Give your kid support and guidance

You'll find thought-provoking questions for reflection—or to discuss in small groups with other parents. Gain a fresh understanding of how you can help your teenager develop into a healthy, Christian adult!

Family Tree ISBN 0-931529-83-2 199 pages $9.95

PARENTING TEENAGERS

Video kit

Get the insights and encouragement you need to cope with your teenagers from Parenting Teenagers. You'll discover practical communication tips, the whys of rebellion, insights on mood swings, ideas for handling peer pressure . . . plus parenting styles, kids' friends and more . . .

Video 1: What Makes Your Teenager Tick?
Video 2: Parenting: How Do You Rate?
Video 3: Communicating With Your Teenager
Video 4: Your Teenager's Friends and Peer Pressure

Watch **Parenting Teenagers** at home, or use for years to come in parents meetings, retreats or Sunday school.

Your complete kit includes four 30-minute VHS videos and 144-page information-packed leaders guide full of helpful, ready-to-copy worksheets.

Group Books   ISBN 0-931529-60-3   Video kit $98

HELPING YOUR TEENAGER SUCCEED IN SCHOOL

by Dorothy and Lyle Williams

Discover how to help your teenager get more out of school. Plus, how to help your teenager:

- Build self-esteem
- Accept responsibility
- Cope with school pressures, and more

You'll learn how to be a positive role model for your young people, encourage your kid to learn, and see grades and school from a Christian perspective.

Family Tree   ISBN 0-931529-63-8   190 pages $8.95

WHAT MAKES YOUR TEENAGER TICK

by Dr. G. Keith Olson

Here's practical Christian help for every parent who has ever been baffled by their teenager's behavior. With this easy-to-read guide you'll learn to bring out the best in your kid. You'll explore your teenager's personality, plus how to react, how to discipline and how to nurture.

Learn to better understand your teenager. And through understanding, your family can build strong, positive relationships—to last a lifetime.

Adapted from the best-selling book *Why Teenagers Act the Way They Do.*

Family Tree   ISBN 0-931529-75-1   216 pages $8.95

FIXING YOUR FRAZZLED FAMILY

By Dean Feldmeyer

Group®
Loveland, Colorado

Fixing Your Frazzled Family

First Printing

Credits
Edited by Eugene C. Roehlkepartain
Cover and book designed by Judy Atwood Bienick
Illustrations by Steve Elde

Library of Congress Cataloging-in-Publication Data
Feldmeyer, Dean, 1951-
Fixing your frazzled family / by Dean Feldmeyer.
p. cm.
ISBN 0-931529-98-0
1. Family—United States—Psychological aspects. 2. Stress (Psychology) 3. Parenting—Religious aspects—Christianity. 4. Teenagers—United States—Family relationships. I. Title.
HQ536.F44 1990
306.85'0973—dc20 89-25718
CIP

Printed in the United States of America